Buxtonians
A NEVER ENDING STORY

Written and Published by Yvonne Eyre Chalker

Copyright 2020

ISBN No. 978-0-9525288-5-2

Design and Print by Printexpress (Buxton) Ltd
The Old Schoolhouse, Market Street, Buxton SK17 6LD

ENJOY YOUR DREAM BEFORE IT TURNS INTO A NIGHTMARE

Yvonne Eyre Chalker

'On two occasions I was asked: 'Is there going to be a Buxtonians II?' If so, they would like to contribute. I was hooked. As before, the book has evolved and taken its own path.

March 2020: Literally overnight I am changing direction with my introduction. Buxtonians, like the rest of the world face the unprecedented Corona (covid) virus. True to form we come up trumps with our hardy spirit and yet again proud to be Buxtonian.'

Front cover

Twins, Constance and Annie Allpress. Constance and Annie were born in Fairfield 1899. At the start of the twentieth century their family home was: 1, Westmoreland Villas, Fairfield Road.

Jo Shoebridge

'My Dad was manager of W. H. Smith, The Colonnade, Buxton in the late 1960s. The lovely ladies, Connie and Annie, worked for him and were long serving news-delivery girls. Dad says "They did the longest newspaper rounds with a smile, rarely seen apart, and it was very difficult to be sure which one you were talking to! Always laughing and, very proud to tell you, they had been interviewed on local BBC television, telling of their many years of "news delivery service".'

Facebook Responses

Kenneth Lees

'Didn't chat to you much but always had that beaming smile for you.'

Judith Gardner

'I remember them very well; they were always dressed exactly the same usually in bright colours.'

Pauline Lowe

'I would see them regularly playing tennis in Ashwood Park.'

Back cover

Kevin Hall was born in Buxton at 101 Fairfield Road. He has lived and worked here all his life.

He has always been proud of his home town but alas, over the last few years, due to cut backs etc. he has noticed a decline.

Rather than sit back, he took it upon himself to tidy up the Market Place, when necessary. Lucky for me he did.

One Sunday morning, I realised my phone was mislaid from the previous night. Panic! A little later my land line rang. It was my daughter. "Mum" she said. "A Mr Hall has phoned me. He saw my number on your phone. He has found it on the Market Place! Thank You Kevin!

Snippet

The pet shop, Nature's Own in the background, has been in business for 40 years. Stuart Ellison and his family set up their first shop on Ash Street. They were there for a short while before moving to Number 1 High Street.

Martin Elvin

Dennis Elvin spent his formative years in the sleepy village of Peak Dale before moving to the bright lights of Buxton.

Dennis' work life was that of an electric engineer, starting at Ferodo, before moving to Otter Controls, where he would stay for the best part of 30 years. Juxtaposed to his working disciplines, he always had a creative flair. Dennis would while away his free time in artistic endeavours, painting, sketching, etching etc.

At Otter Controls his creative talents were soon engaged by ways of cartoons in the quarterly newsletter. These were typical caricatures of some of the many "characters" who have worked at "Otters" over the years. From this, perhaps it was a natural progression to his providing regular cartoons for the local newspaper. Over the years Dennis provided numerous illustrations, partly poking fun at local issues and politics. Car parking and the Crescent were always fair game!

These cartoons were widely well received and often one of the first things the reader would turn to. Not all of his efforts were published. Some were rejected without explanation. Perhaps too controversial or political!

IT WOULD SEEM THAT THE CONTROLLED PARKING SCHEME IS NOW IN OPERATION.

ITS DICK WHITTINGTON. HE THINKS BUXTON MARKET PLACE IS PAVED WITH GOLD.

George Critchlow born 1814, here with his daughter Elizabeth.
They lived at Rose Cottage, Chelmorton.

Ann Gibbs

My Great, Great, Great-grand-father was born in Monyash in 1779. He used the surnames Morewood and also Critchlow. Family Marriages and baptisms are recorded using both surnames. I believe his father was William Morewood, born 1736, and there are several explanations for the change of name. It had been romantically thought to be in order to receive a legacy, on the condition that the family used the name Critchlow!

Daniel was a master Cordwainer (shoemaker) and raised 17 children, all of whom became shop owners, farmers or held similar jobs. There are understandably a great number of his descendants around, spread over the area, including Bakewell, Tideswell and Buxton.

Daniel's son George, born 1814, lived in Chelmorton with his wife Elizabeth (nee Needham). He was a great character, famed for his extremely long walks, and lived to almost 100 years old. He also used the surname Walker from time to time! Their son Henry, born 1854 in Chelmorton, moved to Buxton and worked as a cab driver from the St. Anne's stable on Palace Road, where Buxton Press is now.

Henry married Mary (Polly) Coates, and by all accounts she was a battle-axe. Her favourite trick, to unnerve company, was to turn her glass eye the wrong way round!

Henry's son, Thomas Henry, was born in Buxton in 1893 and lived here all his life. As a young child he washed bottles at the Sun Inn on High Street, standing on a crate to reach the sink. His mother was widowed and left with a family to raise and the boys must have been a trial to her – they were full of mischief, and he and his brother George told me many tales of their exploits.

Thomas Henry

Thomas Henry was a sergeant in WWI in the Army Service Corps, after which I believe he was a driver in Buxton. He married Nellie Huxtable from Cornwall and they lived on West Road.

George also served in WWI and as a young man had been Head Porter at the prestigious Palace Hotel having worked his way up from a page boy. He and Thomas Henry bought a garage on West Road, selling petrol, running taxis, offering car repairs and garaging space etc., which he was involved in until Thomas died in 1954. Thomas had also branched out into the undertaking business, buying Peter Bennett's at 24 High Street in the early 1940s. We lived on the premises which are now a part of the news agency on High Street, until his illness in about 1953. Thomas and Nellie's son, George, married my mother Alice Lomax, from Sheffield, and sadly, she and my twin both died when I was born. I was brought up mainly by my grandparents.

George married Margaret (Peggy) Kay, and had three more children: Thomas, Marian and Graham. Thomas died as a young boy, Marian moved to the Isle Of Man but is now back in Derbyshire with her son Tom. Graham still lives in the town and raised his family here.

I was born here, in the St. John's Nursing Home, which is just around the corner from where I now live. My schooling was at Hardwick Square, then Cavendish Girls' School and I have many happy memories of both. I have worked mainly in Buxton as, after short spells away in the Civil Service and for a while, in Stockport, my working life has been in Buxton.

In 1961 I married Stuart Gibbs, a Buxton man. We raised our three children; Andrew, Sarah and Emma here. Two of them still live in the town and one in Glossop. And four of our grandchildren still live here whilst one lives in Glossop. We are truly a Derbyshire family – and for five generations, Buxtonians!

Snippet

As a child Ann, living on High Street, would take her Grandad, Tommy Critchlow's collar's to Tong Youe the owner of the Chinese Laundry at 12, High Street.

Mr Tong Youe would always greet her by saying "You come for little fat man's collars"...

Mr Tong Youe had a brother. After the second World War they worked hard, saving enough money for them and their families to return home to China.

Mr Tong Youe would have had strong competition from the family run IXL Laundry.

Thomas Bagguley and his wife Emma, moved to Buxton from Nottinghamshire at the end of the 19th century.

To earn a living they started a laundry business at Laundry Cottage, Fairfield. By 1908 their address was 71 Queens Road and Fairfield Laundry.

After two failed attempts, he would be assisted by his three sons, Francis Leonard, Thomas Henry and Percy Gerald, known as Mr Frank, Mr Tommy and Mr Percy. Proving to be third time lucky. By 1925 business had expanded and moved to their own work premises on Charles Street.

In the 1970s Later IXL moved to Bridge Street. IXL The management at this time was Thomas Bagguley and his cousins David and Peter Bagguley. By 2000 the laundry building had been demolished and made way for housing.

Peter Bagguley met Eileen Moss when she was 11 unknown to them, they would later marry.

As a girl Eileen lived on London Road and went to Hardwick Square School. She learnt to roller skate in Mug's Alley. Mug's Alley apparently was situated at the side of the Octagon which was accessed from steps down from St. John's Road. Another recollection was the Rat Catcher up and down the town alleyways.

During the Second World War, her family home was spacious. Like all spacious houses in the town, they were asked by the authorities, to take in fleeing Jewish Refugees escaping persecution.

Immediately Eileen struck up a rapport with the Jewish visitors, not only the family living with them but other Jewish families.

Peter and Eileen married early on a Saturday morning at 10.00am. Followed by a reception held upstairs at the Manchester Arms. Elsie Salt wife of the landlord Arthur was Eileen's aunt. Later the Blazing Rag would be the venue for both their children's Christening "Do's".

Arthur Salt became Mayor of Buxton in 1950.

Seventy three years later the Blazing Rag is run by Elsie's Great, Great Nephew Craig Hodgkinson and his partner Lisa.

Fairfield Stud Farm

Helen Plowes

James Plowes was born in Hook, Hampshire, 1860. When James was twenty one he was working as a groom at Waterton Hall, Garthorpe. Whilst driving coaches to Buxton, which he regularly did, James met Dr Hazelwood, a surgeon whose great interest was breeding horses.

Dr Hazelwood owned Fairfield Stud Farm where many well-known horses had been bred and shown all over the country.

When James was 26, Dr Hazelwood offered him the job of Stud Groom. He accepted, bringing Anne Marie, his wife, and young daughter, Elsie May to Town End, Fairfield. He soon progressed, becoming Stud Manager.

James, and Anne Marie had five more children, all christened at St Peter's Church, Fairfield. They were George, James, Harry, Arthur Edward and Mary Elizabeth (Madge).

The two older boys, George and James, would share their father's interest of horses. Both moved to live and work in Newmarket, Suffolk.

By 1904 the family were living at Fairfield stud farm, Dr Hazlewood having moved to live on Terrace Road.

In 1917 Buxton Lime Firms bought the stud with James continuing as manager. James re-bought the Stud Farm in 1924.

James and Anne Marie's third son, Harry, were born in 1891. Harry, sometimes known as Dill, went to Fairfield school where he completed his education. On leaving school he had a pony and trap, selling apples and fish in the village. He then got an apprenticeship with Tom Lomas, a local farrier.

When the First World War broke out in 1914, a big recruiting campaign was held, from which many local young men joined up. Harry, by then had completed his apprenticeship and enlisted with the Royal Veterinary Corps. He spent the whole war in Mesopotamia as a blacksmith. Harry's favourite personal horse was Daisy. Daisy was his transport, taking Harry wherever he was needed.

On his return from the War, Harry went to work for Arnold Firth, Farrier and Wheelwright whose Smithy was in Lower Fairfield. Harry also started a tennis club in a field behind the Stud. The field, situated on the side of a hill, needed constant levelling, to enable a good playing surface.

Harry met Elsie Dawson, (a native of Buxton). They married on 9th June 1926 at Buxton Congregational Church, Hardwick Street. Their home was 2, Stonecliffe Terrace, Fairfield.

The following year Harry's father James died, leaving all his property to his wife Anne Marie, including the Stud farm.

Arnold Firth's Smithy. Arnold Firth and Harry Plowes on the left.

Harry rented the forge on the Stud farm but by 1929 Harry and his brother had gone into business, buying the forge between them.

Harry and Elsie's first child was David Dawson Plowes, born 1927, followed by Norman "Harry", 1928. Both children were born at Stonecliffe Terrace.

In 1932 Harry and Elsie bought Fairfield Villa, a larger house with outbuildings where Harry could have his forge, petrol pumps and later, a pigeon loft. Here he kept his prize birds which would fly all over the South of England and even to France.

The house was also convenient to have elderly relatives to live and stay when they could no longer cope alone.

Their only daughter, Dorothy Elsie, was born on 7th March 1934. They were a very close knit family, enjoying many outings together.

Before the Second World War started, Harry and Elsie opened a cigarette and confectionery shop in their front room, to particularly cater for the early morning trade; quarry workers, I.C.I. and the Basalt Works.

All went well until rationing started, after which it was difficult to keep afloat. Harry continued his work as a Blacksmith. He would walk many a mile, carrying his tools to his customers who lived far and wide in the villages around Buxton.

Of course, many people would bring their horses to Harry's forge, where he had all the traditional equipment.

Because of his long association with horses, Harry was well known for his skill in the treatment of ailments and accurate diagnoses, particularly in the case of leg problems. Indeed, the last case he undertook was a nasty leg infection which baffled the vets for a long while but for which Harry was able to prescribe a cure. Many of his treatments were age-old recipes made from homeopathic ingredients.

When at last the time came for retirement, about 1950, Harry and Elsie moved into the Nook, Dakin Avenue. This was an old house,

Harry and Elsie Plowes, with their children Dorothy, David and Norman.

adjoining the garden of Fairfield Villa. It had originally been bought by Tom Dawson, Elsie's father.

The main part dated back to the 13th century and had enormously thick walls.

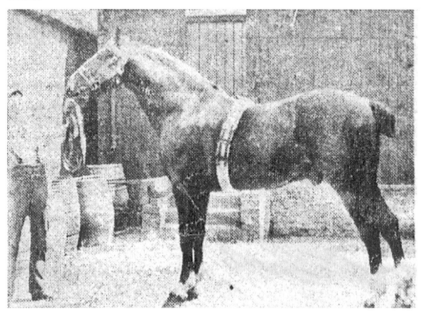

Travelling day at stud farm.

"Buxton Advertiser" Letters page, date unknown, referring to Fairfield Stud Farm.

Eric Ashmore, 10 Princes Road.

'As a schoolboy I well remember the 'Entires' being given exercise on Fairfield Common. These consisted of Hunters, Hackney Ponies and Shirehorse Stallions. They were exercised on a long leather lunge line, running in circles. They attended, and always won prizes, at the London Horse Show, travelling to London by rail horse box. We used to meet them on their return to see the premiums and cups they had won. This helped them to travel and serve during the year in various parts of the country. Here are a few of the people I remember who worked at the Stud:

Mr Plowes Snr; George Plowes; Jim Plowes; Harry Plowes; Hilda Plowes; Mabel Plowes; Mary Plowes; Mr Fowler; Mr Morton; Charlie Thomas;

Dan Austin; Len Austin; George Weston; "Stallion" Jack Swann; Mr Dawson; Arthur Wooliscroft; Fred Lomas; Harry Morton Jnr and Freddy Lomas Jnr.'

Len Austin could recite the pedigree of every stallion in the Stud. Buxton Lime Firms took over and bred Suffolk Punches.

H. Norton, Chaddesden, Derby

My father, who will be remembered by many, worked for Dr Hazlewood and Mr Plowes Senior. He also went on to work for Jim Plowes Junior. There have been many comments about Dr Hazlewood in your paper. As a boy, what I remember of him was the Oxo tin he carried, which was always full of humbugs. He kept some very good stallions, and was written about by Mr Unwin of Tewkesbury, in the "Horse and Hound".

A few names I remember of thoroughbred stallions are: Cornmint; Braintree; Spearmint and Tidas. Two hackney stallions; Flashaway and Glenavon Torres. I had a ride on the last mentioned while only a schoolboy.

Some Shire stallions also were kept. One I remember was Harold's Heir.

He kept about fourteen in all and the stallions were lunged in those days on Fairfield Common, where Mr Slater kept many sheep at one time.

Yes, they were good days, watching them return from London shows but, better still, when they returned from travelling. My father travelled many counties, a few times in Fifeshire, Scotland, being away all summer. I loved to get down to the stud and listen to Mr Plowes Snr. talking. I thought him great. His son, George, was at Hamilton Stud, Newmarket, which had some very good stallions, one a Derby winner in 1910. I think he was called Lemberg.

Snippet

The 1911 census shows Len Austin aged 29. Occupation, Stud Groom and Horse Keeper. This leads me to believe that the letters written in the "Advertiser" were recalling the Stud Farm around this time.

Entires: Uncastrated male horses.

Lunged: Trained.

THEY ARE UFO'S WHO HAVE LANDED TO REFUEL FROM OUR GAS MAIN.

Torr Street is situated in probably the oldest part of town, with St. Ann's Church close by on Church Street, dating back to c1634.

An 1842 Directory, shows Torr Street with just 6 dwellings.

1. Oldfield, Mr

2. Brunt, Mr Robert

3. Deakin, Mr William. Hyde House.

4. Worrall, Mr

5. Welling, Mr W.H. Manager of the Gentleman Natural Baths

6. Greaves, Mr

Ninety five years later, in the 1937 Kelly's Directory, there are 26 houses and dwellings. It is a typical town street of its time. Mixed amongst the residential houses are: Bennett undertakers; Ben Simpson's boy's club; Sturgess Engineers; Holmes, shopkeeper; Cox shopkeeper; Wm Heathcote joiner (works); J Bootherstone, plumbers; Sutton & Co, carriers; G Parnell, cabinet maker; Mrs Mabel Shirt, upholsterer.

2020 and Torr Street still has working premises.

Today, David Riley (Rice) lives at 9, Torr Street, moving there in 1990. He has in his possession the original parchment house deeds dating back to 1735. To hand he has a will dated and witnessed by George Needham and Joseph Richardson. Rice was born in Buxton on Sherwood Road and has a great interest in the town's local history and characters. He has an allotment on Cote Heath and the ground rent is still paid to the Duke of Devonshire's estate.

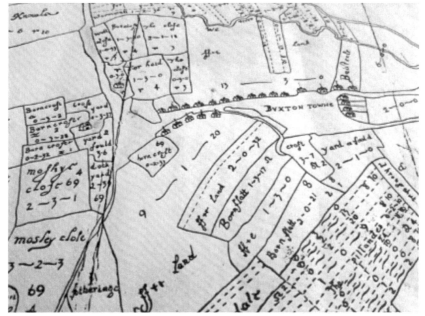

On the map is written: 'Surveyed by Mr Senior upon the scale of 16 poles in a inch in the yeare of our Lord God 1631.'

Business on Torr Street

Steve Drabble

As a school boy my Grandad Robert (Bob) Drabble had an interest in woodwork and was making decorative radio fronts for Watson's radio shop, on Terrace Road, with a peddle powered Fret Saw in the loft of his home.

He started an apprenticeship as a cabinet maker in the early 1930s for Parnell's Furniture Makers situated in Parnell's Yard on Torr Street which is now Torr Street Mews.

I believe he started his joinery business before the Second World War, however, during the war he was sent around the country building

Mulberry harbours before going off to war himself.

After the war he started his business, R. F. Drabble - Joiner and Cabinet Maker, and in 1963 he rented a first floor workshop on Torr Street (now No. 26) which was next to where he started his apprenticeship.

In 1968 my dad Peter went into partnership with my grandad and in 1976 they moved into what was formerly Ben Simpson's Gymnasium. In more recent times we have also moved into the building next door which has previously been a Boys Club, an undertakers mortuary and coffin workshop, Joe Rose Fabrics and Brindley Bros Painters and Decorators.

My grandad started and finished on Torr Street, my dad started and will finish on Torr Street it looks like it will be the same for myself.

Snippet

The opposite side of Torr Street stood another long standing family business, Yates Garage.

On the three street corners, Cox's, Drabble's and Mrs Goodwin's. If one shop did not have what you were after, one of the others would come to your rescue.

Hardwick Square School 1888/1889. Oliver's father, Arthur Gomersal is 3rd from right in the 2nd row up.

Oliver Gomersal

My grandfather Ernest Gomersal came to Buxton in 1888. He was supervisor for the firm of Naylor Bros which built railways and were contracted to build the Buxton to Ashbourne line.

His family lived on West Road in what would be a new house in those days. After completing the line as far as Parsley Hay, the family moved to Ashbourne from where they linked up the line to Parsley Hay.

The last railway job his firm did was in Ireland, during the First World War. After which he retired to his native Yorkshire. As a small boy I remember that when he came to visit us in Buxton, he always had to go and see Dukes Drive Viaduct, of which he was rightly proud.

Arthur Gomersal, Ernest's son was described in his obituary as perhaps the most colourful character in the town during the first half of the 1900s. In the Edwardian period he was captain and secretary of the local football club, and opening bat for the Buxton cricket team. He was also well known in the town as a singer and an entertainer.

Later in life he had made one of the finest private collections of paintings in the town, which were, on several occasions, exhibited at the local Art Gallery which now owns most of them. He was also a man who enjoyed natural beauty, being particularly fond of the Lake District.

Arthur married Gertrude who was a pianist and it is against this sporting and artistic background that their children, Margaret and her elder brother, 'me', grew up.

Margaret Wood, nee Gomersal, was born at Buxton in March 1924. After attending the Buxton elementary school she became a pupil at the local secondary school, where her sporting abilities became evident. She excelled at tennis and hockey and, as a senior pupil, was invited to join the Buxton Hockey Team, the most prestigious team in the area.

Later she became a member of one of the two Buxton tennis clubs, appearing regularly in the ladies first team and at one period, the ladies captain.

Likewise, she also became a member of the Badminton clubs in Buxton, and she and her partner were a formidable pair in the district.

At the age of 15 she started to make a scrapbook of newspaper cuttings and illustrations which covered the first year and a half of the War, and this is now in the collection of the "Museum of Childhood" at Sudbury Hall in Derbyshire. Upon leaving school she joined the staff of the local solicitor's firm, Brooke-Taylor. After some years she became the secretary of Col E. M. Brooke Taylor the head of the firm and also the father of Tim Brooke-Taylor of T.V. fame, "The Goodies".

She later specialised in testamentary matters and represented the firm in the execution of provisions of Wills after the testator had died. At the time of her marriage she was also the deputy Registrar for Buxton.

In 1951, in the window of a motor cycle shop in Buxton there appeared something altogether new - a VESPA SCOOTER, the first one to be seen in the town. This rather took her eye and she said to her brother Oliver, "Do you think that I could learn to ride that?" He of course, replied "Yes, and what is more, if you are really interested in it - I will go halves with you". So she was probably the first woman "scooterist" in the town! Quite in keeping with the family tradition as her maternal grandmother was one of the first lady cyclists in Buxton. One of the other well-known solicitors in town would refer to Margaret as "Miss Gomersal on her buzz bomb".

It was on a scooter trip to relatives at Chadwell near Melton Mowbray that she met Sydney who was also there on a visit. They were married in late December 1964.

Oliver and his wife Marjorie always enjoyed a visit to Newark where the landscape is so different from their native Peak District and of course Margaret and Sydney often visited Buxton.

Katherine Hepburn (movie star) on an early 1950s Vespa scooter built in England, called the Douglas.

Margaret developed a hobby of making high class doll's clothes for the "Cindy" range and these were sold at the Newark Oxfam where Margaret helped, for quite some years. She was a keen photographer in the period when transparencies were fashionable and sometimes, she would show her photographs of her and Sydney's Mediterranean, Continental and Canadian holidays, at ladies club meetings.

After Sydney's death she became more active as a gardener and at one time had an interesting and colourful collection of Cacti of various "shapes and spikes".

As she got older her activities were curtailed but she was always a keen reader until, with failing eyesight this became difficult, but she was able to enjoy television until almost her final illness.

I (Oliver Gomersal) was born on 21st May 1921. After infant school I went to Kents Bank School from which scholarship to Buxton College. Reasonably good at Cricket I made the grade for the College 1st eleven. Two members of the team became lifelong friends of mine... Harold Barstow and Ken Lowndes.

Margaret and Oliver, 1940.

On leaving school I went to an uncle in Teddington on Thames who had a small printing works. I attended Twickenham Technical College and studied the history of printing, lettering and layout. In 1939 the outbreak of war caused the printing works to close due to a shortage of paper. On my return home I was lucky enough to get a job at Buxton town hall in the Treasurer's Department.

In 1940 I joined the Home Guard (Dad's Army) which was very useful pre-military training. July 1941 I joined the RAF for training as an observer (Air navigator and bomb aimer). Main flying training was done in South Africa at Oudtshoorn which is the centre of the Ostrich farming industry, very popular with present day tourists.

After returning to England I went on a specialist course at Squires Gate (Blackpool) airport for work in Coastal Command and cooperation with the Navy. From here we went to Siloth in the Solway Firth to "crew up" and learn to fly in Wellington aircraft. This was a ten week course, flying out in the North Atlantic. After completing this course, we were posted to a new squadron being formed in East Africa, to patrol the NW area of the Indian Ocean and Gulf of Aden.

621 Squadron was formed to counter the increased submarine activity in the North West part of the Indian Ocean, when the Mediterranean and Suez Canal opened again for ships going to India, Burma and Ceylon. 16 crews flew their Wellington bomber aircraft out to East Africa in August and September 1943. We flew across the Bay of Biscay at dead

of night, to avoid German fighter planes, then over the Atlas mountains to Libya and on to Cairo. Here we stayed a few days before flying down the Nile Valley to Khartoum, then on to touch the Northern tip of Lake Victoria before landing in Kenya at Nairobi. We then flew north to Mogadishu in Somalia which would be the Squadron's headquarters for the next 3 months before moving to Aden our main base'.

We flew from desert airstrips on the Horn of Africa and from the island of Socotoa 200 miles out in the Indian ocean.

Of the 16 crews who flew their aircraft out only 12 crews ever returned.

In my own crew four of us lived to be in our nineties, but sadly our pilot who had been awarded the Distinguished Flying Cross for a successful attack we made on a German Submarine, was killed in an air accident in 1945 (and the shock killed his Mother).

Wellington bombers.

All our flying was done under "wireless silence" except for emergencies. I did all the navigations by now, old fashioned "Dead Reckoning" on charts, mathematically. For me the flight out to Kenya was the "Trip of a Lifetime", the average height the planes flew at was 3,000 feet. The average height in 2020 is 31,000 to 38,000 feet.

I was flying with another crew whilst their navigator was sick, when we found a boat and raft with survivors from a torpedoed ship. We were able to get them picked up by the Navy (for information about the mission, see 'Search for Survivors of SS Tarifa in the Indian Ocean'. bbc.uk/history/ww2peopleswar/stories/). Also whilst flying with my own crew we depth-charged a German submarine which had just dived, and forced it to the surface. It was eventually captured and a lot of intelligence material was obtained. Our Captain and front gunner were decorated for the affair.

After completing a year in East Africa and the Indian Ocean I returned to the UK where I attended a special centre for Transport Command work which was then expanding, to do with the safe loading of aircraft, as regards the centre of gravity and weight, and the handling of passengers and freight.

After appointments at three airfields in the UK, I was posted to Copenhagen, Prague, and Singapore from where I was shipped home for demobilisation, leaving with the rank of Flight Lieutenant.

In Autumn 1946, I resumed my job in the Treasurer's department in a new "Costing Office", furnishing costs on the various jobs undertaken by the council's road maintenance teams plus all the work on maintenance of all the various buildings owned by the council (Town Hall, Pavilion Gardens, Baths, Sewage, Waterworks and all the council houses). The Gas Works and Electricity undertakings were nationalised the next year. All this work was carried out by the Buxton Surveyors Department.

In 1963 I moved to the Highways Department on Market Street and put in charge of the Office and Highway Stores for 8 years, a very interesting part of the job because this was where it was all happening.

I always considered myself very lucky to have married my wife, Marjorie who was known and loved by such a wide circle of people until her death in 2008. We enjoyed interesting holidays all over England, Scotland and Wales, being members of both the National Trust and English Heritage. A recent check revealed that we had visited over 120 of the National Trust venues, many of them on more than one occasion.

1971 saw me returning to the Surveyors Department as Chief Clerk until local government reorganisation in 1974, when I became a senior administrator in the Technical Services Department which dealt with similar work over all the newly grouped North Derbyshire towns of "Borough of the High Peak" and taking retirement in 1979.

After playing tennis in Buxton local parks I became a member (and later Treasurer) of the Buxton Gardens Lawn Tennis Club situated at the end of the promenade and now a car park. One year my partner and I won the mixed doubles cup.

During this period I was a member of the main committee of the Buxton Lawn Tennis Championships, held on both grass and hard courts in the Pavilion Gardens, for their last two years; it finished, I think in 1954, due to rapidly mounting expenses.

At this time I was also a member of the Buxton Spa Table Tennis club. There was a thriving North Derbyshire table tennis league at the time. In 1951, for a holiday, I walked to London with an ex RAF friend, starting from Dove Dale. This was one of the most interesting weeks I ever spent.

On the horticultural side, I helped my father with his large allotment on Crowestones, taking it over after he died, for seven years. When I later went to live on Mosley Road I managed to have a good floral display in containers and troughs both at the front and sides of the house and on the back patio, many of the flowers being grown by me, from seed.

In 1980, I was invited to join the Buxton Archaeological Society where I was eventually made a life member in 2012. I addressed the society on a number of occasions and contributed from time to time to the periodical newsletter which was started during my term as Chairman.

I had a particular interest in Buxton history, especially the development of our local government, from the first Local Board in 1859. The late Mr Glyn Jones, C.E. of Borough of High Peak, kindly gave me access to the early records. My most important work was to make a study of the subscribers to the Buxton Ballroom in the Crescent from when it opened in 1788 until its final year in 1840. No one else seems to have done it in the detail I went to, so I like to think I have made a reasonable contribution to Buxton history.

In 1986, I met Mike Langham and Colin Wells who had just completed their first book "Buxton Waters" in typescript. They asked me to read their draft in case they had made any statements at which older Buxton residents would raise their eyebrows. This was the start of a happy and fruitful relationship which included their next six books or so. We were all delighted when Mike was awarded a doctorate in local history, and saddened by his early death.

When the Neighbourhood Watch Scheme was set up I was the representative of Mosley Road for the first 10 years, passing it on when I was 80 years of age- quite an interesting job.

1990 I was invited to join the committee of "The Friends of Buxton Cottage Hospital" on which I served for a number of years, helping with the various "efforts" to raise money and at one time I was Chairman. This brought me a whole new spectrum of friends of course.

Because of my knowledge of local history I have been consulted for various local publications from 1984 to 2020, for which due acknowledgement was printed.

I now find that at the age of 99, I am consulted for my memory, from 1925 to the present day.

Snippet

What needs pointing out about Mr Gomersal is that he is a 99 year old Gentleman with a unique and wry sense of humour.

Buxton Park Superintendents

Oliver Gomersal

As Buxton expanded after being combined with Fairfield to form the Borough of Buxton in 1917 the Parks Superintendent was eventually responsible for the various parks in the town, the Serpentine, the Slopes, Ashwood Park, Cote Heath Park and Recreation Ground and the park at Fairfield, but the Pavilion Gardens being a centre of attraction for the visitors (who paid to get in) was regarded as being the most important of his duties.

During the Victorian period there was a well known superintendent who was known universally as "Head Gardener Hogg and his name is always connected with the Pavilion Gardens of that period. He lived in a house somewhere in the Gardens that would have been roughly at the rear of the present swimming pool.

Mr Tom Ellis arrived in Buxton in the early 1920s. Although he originated from the Southampton area he had in his youth been in South Africa and used to say that he had watered the plants and trees in tubs on Adderly Street, the main street in Capetown. No doubt he was one of the young men who returned to England to take part in the First World War. He lived in Serpentine House and oversaw the management of the nurseries adjacent, which is now Serpentine Community Garden Society.

He retired in the late 1950s to be replaced by Mr Jim Boyle. He came to Buxton from Blackpool where he had been in charge of some large nurseries. He was responsible for planting all the croci on the slopes- originally a mass of colour much talked about at the time.

Also during his period of office, on the well known BBC radio programme "Gardener's Question Time", one of the resident experts. Bill Sowerbutts remarked on a very fine "Star of Bethlehem" to be seen in Buxton's Pavilion Gardens.

Mr Boyle left Buxton to take a post in charge of the parks and gardens in Penzance thus creating some sort of record by moving from the holiday town with one of coldest climate in England to one of the warmest. He remarked before his departure that he would have to "revise" on his sub-tropical plants.

He was succeeded by a man named Frank More who at one time had been in charge of an estate in Wiltshire contiguous with the National

Trust property Laycock Abbey and the Fox Talbot Photography Museum. He didn't stay very long being replaced by Mr Fred Thorley who came to Buxton from the immaculate Trentham Gardens in the late 1960s.

The swimming pool was built during his period of office and he was responsible for the bank of blossom trees and flowering shrubs behind it, bordering on St Johns Road. He made the comment that when you set out a new area with trees and shrubs you should if possible visit it every four or five years to see if it had developed as you had envisaged it. He was also the creator of some small beds at the bottom of the slopes of intricate designs or slogans in bedding plants. He left Buxton about 1975 to go to Staines in Middlesex where he reported that amongst his responsibilities was one of the banks of the River Thames.

The 1974 Local Government Reorganization brought to Buxton the superintendent from Glossop, Mr Walter Waterworth, as Director of Amenities. He was both well qualified with the "Diploma of the Parks and Recreation Administration" and was very artistic in person.

He built some rosebeds on the promenade, alongside the swimming pool. Amongst his other activities he had some trees and shrubs cut down so that from the high point near the sunken walk from Broad Walk to Burlington Road there was a striking view to the Old Hall which no one had seen for years. It was probably during his term of office that the children's railway was introduced.

He retired in 1978 and was replaced by a lady who was a specialist in children's play equipment, She had to rely heavily on the Assistant Superintendents of Glossop and Buxton for the horticultural work in the parks and Pavilion Gardens.

She moved on after a comparatively short time and Buxton's parks and Pavilion Gardens were left in the hands of Stephen Lobb who had come to Buxton from Southend. When he retired it coincided with the fashion in local government for various activities to be put in the hands of outside contractors, thus reducing the number of people employed directly by local authorities.

Christina Hewitt

My mother and I were the first people to move into Haddon Road... it was 1938. We moved in after my father, Arnold Potts, had just died of double pneumonia. I was 2 years old.

The total cost of the mortgage my Mum had to pay was £500. The houses on Haddon Road were built by a builder called Royle, who lived at number 81 Victoria Park Road, in a house he had built for himself. It is still my home and the place I raised my four sons, Glenn, Mark, Peter, and Kevin.

My mother was a dressmaker and tailoress. She learned to sew in London at a high class firm called Bradleys.

She had to work very hard at dressmaking just to make ends meet. A man used to come on a bike with a basket on the front, full of clothes for my Mum to make or alter. I remember that one of my Mum's regular customers was old Mrs Morris from Morris's fishmongers, a local firm still going to this day.

The material and clothes that my Mum worked on came from a shop called Holmes, a gentleman's outfitters on Spring Gardens. The shop was later a Wimpey bar and is now The Hydro. I remember going with my Mum and calling in at the shop to collect her wages. When she bought any cottons or other sewing supplies, the man in the shop would put the money she paid into a tin, put the lid on tight, and then send the tin up a chute to the cashier, who would then send the tin back with the change in. As a little girl, I used to be fascinated watching the tin whizzing up and down the chute with the money in. Nowadays the ordinary shop tills are nothing like as fascinating.

When I was a girl, if you had any room in your house you had to take in refugees. We took in a lot of different people to help pay for the rent. This meant that my bed was often two chairs put together, I used to think it was great.

Mrs Morris.

One time we had two girls from the pantomime staying with us and I went to see the show they were in. Before the show, they took me in to the dressing rooms, so I could see where they got changed in to their costumes and put their make up on. Watching the show later, I was really thrilled to think that they were staying in our house.

When I was older I used to play with my friends on the rough land at the bottom of Haddon Road where the council houses are now. We called it 'the clods'. Around bonfire night, we would build a big bonfire on the clods using sticks and branches that we had collected from the wood down the hill, above Ashwood Park. I remember the wood was called 'Monkey Wood'. Other times we used to sledge down the big hill when there was lots of snow. Often I would go round to visit my auntie, my Mum's sister, who lived in the red house on Windsor Road. I loved it there. I used to try to mow the lawn for her, but it was very hard going. Then my auntie bought a goat to keep the grass down. We learned to milk the goat. My auntie also kept chickens and we would collect the eggs. I remember the cat having kittens and there were little yellow fluffy chicks everywhere too. My auntie loved to keep animals and I loved it too. My auntie was a milliner and had a shop on Fairfield Road.

My uncle was Reg Bainbridge. His father used to do the funerals. Another of his jobs was taking trippers up to the Cat and Fiddle. My uncle would have to get the horses ready, and shine the horse brasses.

Uncle Reg fought in the Second World War. One day he happened to come across his brother-in-law at a bar in France. They were really excited and said how wonderful it was to see each other so far away from home and they had their photograph taken together. Mr and Mrs Thorpe lived opposite my aunts red house on Windsor Road. They had a shop at the bottom of Fairfield Road opposite Ashwood Park. Near them lived a lady called Mrs McKinley who was very good at roller skating. In those days people could go roller skating at the gardens and Mrs McKinley used to still go there roller skating when she was in her 60s and 70s. On a Saturday we would go roller skating. Harry Swindells was the man in charge of the roller skates and he was the father of my best friend, Rita.

I remember there were two families that lived next door to one another on Cliff Road, the Coates and the Robinsons. They were big families with eight or nine in each. I was an only child and I used to be amazed at how many of them there were and I used to think how nice it must be to have lots of brothers and sisters.

There were twin girls who lived on Fairfield Road. I didn't know their first names, they were a few years older than me, their second name was Allpress. The twins used to deliver the papers from Jackson's paper shop near the dairy and the Church on the right hand side of Fairfield Road. The girls' father was a cobbler and he had a workshop near the Bull's Head. I remember there was a hole in the side of the wall where you could take your shoes and put them through to be mended, and through the hole I used to watch the cobbler working, mending people's shoes.

Jimmy Coxall was a man who lived with his aunt in one of the tall houses on Queens Road. He used to sell cigarettes and sweets from his bedroom on the first floor of the house to make money. One day my auntie Madge asked me to go and buy her some cigarettes. She meant me to go to the local shop, but instead, for some unknown reason, I went up the stairs in the tall house to Jimmy Coxall. I felt a bit foolish when I realised I had gone to the wrong place.

I had a friend called Yvonne who lived near me on Haddon Road and one day she took me to see where her grandfather worked. He used to have a little bakery on Fairfield Road at the back of the tall houses, down some steps into the cellar. I went there with my friend and saw the place where her grandfather had a big oven that he used for baking pies. He was called Mr Garside and he was quite a plump man, his stomach was so big that he couldn't reach to tie his shoe laces, so Yvonne used to the tie them for him. He used to put together a big tray of pies and then carry the tray on his head over to the Prince of Wales pub at the bottom of Fairfield Road, to sell them.

There was a lady who lived with her mother and sister at Cockeram's Corner who used to do hair-dressing . My mother and auntie used to go there to have their hair done. The first time I had a perm was with Miss Cockeram, one of the daughters, who had set up a hairdressing shop down on Bridge Street. In those days they used to use enormous hair dryers that went over your whole head.

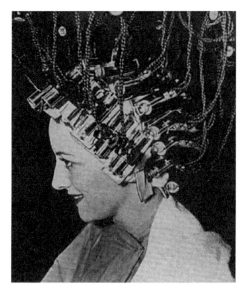

Example 1940s / 1950s Perm.

I was sitting in the shop having my perm done with the dryer over my head when there was an electrical storm, with lots of thunder and lightning. I remember being really frightened that it might strike and electrocute me. It was enough to make my hair curl on its own!

There have been ten different families living next door. The only other original occupant on Haddon Road is John Lomas.

"ITS RUMOURED THAT THERE'S A VACANT CUBICLE AT SYLVAN PARK TOILETS"

THAT REMINDS ME - WE ARE HAVING MEAT AND TWO VEG BOIL IN
THE BAG FOR TEA

BRUNSWICK HOUSE

Brunswick House, Hardwick Square East. Built in 1877-78.

Brunswick House 1946: Mrs Clancy 5th from left.
'Fluffy' Hallows, far left.

Buxton Advertiser and List of Visitors
dated Saturday April 27th 1912

Price: One Penny (1d)

Under the heading: Hotels and Hydropathics.

Brunswick Boarding Establishment(Temperance)

Hardwick Square

ELEVATED ON THE MOUNTAIN LIMESTONE

TABLE D'HOTE   SEPARATE TABLES

NEAR BATHS AND GARDENS

HEATED THROUGHOUT

LARGE RECREATION ROOM

BILLIARDS

SPECIAL TERMS FOR WINTER AND PERMANENT RESIDENCE

SPECIAL DIET IF REQUIRED

PROPRIETRESSES: MISSES WRIGHT

In the 1920s this small, well run Private Hotel was regularly advertised in the Buxton local papers of the period. As well as the usual visitors to the town it had quite a number of elderly permanent residents staying there.

Buxton Advertiser and List of Visitors
dated Saturday August 6th 1927

Price: Two Pennies (2d)

THE BRUNSWICK BUXTON

NEAR STATIONS, BATHS AND GARDENS

EXCELLENT ROOMS MODERATE TARIFF

LARGE ENTERTAINING ROOMS

50 BEDROOMS

TELEPHONE: 45

APPLY: MR & MRS S.D. GENT

A Mrs Clancy owned the hotel during the 1930s. By 1939 she acquired a hotel in Southport, but before she could take up residence it was commandeered by the Army. She was not able to leave the Brunswick until 1946.

Marjorie Gomersal was a Receptionist there in 1946.

Over the years many local people worked at the Brunswick. Amongst them was Eddie Lampard's mum, Margaret Isabella Lampard. Eddie's dad, I quote, apparently sang around the traps after the WWII. This gave him the opportunity of recording with professional musicians at the Conference House.

Derbyshire County Council took over the Brunswick building in the late 1950s/1960s.

Jack Longland (later knighted for his services) was head of Derbyshire Education Committee. His idea was to turn it into the Buxton Conference Centre, primarily for holding conferences for teachers and youth leaders.

Mr and Mrs Jones took over the management in 1961. After the death of her husband, Mrs Jones remained the manager until it closed (due to cuts) in 1991. Prior to them moving to Buxton, they worked for Manchester City Council, running a refuge home for orphans and strays.

On closure, some members of staff were deployed to other jobs within

Derbyshire County Council, Buxton Museum being one of them.

Charis House, (Good News Family Care) has been on the site since the Conference House vacated the building.

Conference House Staff (1970s)

Some of the Crew: Leslie Steeples, Edna Philips, Ann Bates, Julie Philips, Jean Lee, Jo Lynch, Jean Hodgkinson. Vera Harrott, Hazel McDonald Margaret Goodwin, Tess Eyre, Teresa McGrath, Daisy Roberts, Romona, Joan Thompson, Marlene Mycock, her daughter Sue and Lesley Wagstaffe.

When Mum was there I think the unknown motto was hard work, fun, and laughter.

ITS A COMPROMISE. INSTEAD OF A 20 METRE MAST THEY HAVE INSTALLED 20 ONE METRE MASTS

I THINK THEY HAVE GONE TOO FAR WITH CONTROLLED PARKING THIS TIME

RICHMOND HOUSE

Richmond House. Right.

Mike and Sue Jordan bought Richmond House, 35 High Street. On receiving the deeds inherited with the building, they discovered that 'Richmond House' was far older than anyone had thought. The earliest deed, dating back to 1793, mentions the name Lord Nathaniel Scarsdale. The second deed mentions him again, also the Right Honourable Nathaniel Curzon.

The Curzon family had lived in Kedleston near Derby since 1297. In 1759, Lord Curzon commissioned the building of Kedleston Hall. Two years later, in 1761, the head of the family acquired the title of Lord Scarsdale.

Since 1793, Richmond House belonged to many people, including a candlewick maker, spinner and brewer.

1st Lord Nathaniel Scarsdale.   *2nd Lord Nathaniel Scarsdale.*

Listings in Buxton Directories revealed:

1908   Mrs Wooliscroft, grocers and confectioners.

1925   Miss Heathcote, grocers

1937   Mrs Isabella Heathcote, baker
         (to become Mayoress in 1964)

Sue and Mike Jordan bought Richmond House in 1980, spending two years renovating the building. They opened their restaurant, naming it 'Nathaniels', after the first inhabitants of the building. Later Sue and Mike relocated to Market Street with Nathaniels.

Their final move was to The George, George Mansions, where they ran one of the best pubs in town. Many would say the best at that time. Covering food, drink, music, bar games etc. A good time was had by all.

Scarsdale Place further along High Street, was built by Lord Scarsdale, a beneficiary of the 1773/'74 Enclosure Award, for Buxton Manor.

Within this building was an Inn known as the White Hart, later the Scarsdale Arms. The pillared entrance is still a prominent feature. Today it is the entrance to Level Two.

In the 1980s the Bus Club moved there when the North Western bus company situated on Eagle Parade had closed down, leaving its premises on Eagle Parade.

James Mottershead

James Mottershead, my Great Grandfather, on my mother's paternal side, came to Buxton from Macclesfield. He opened a shoe shop number 35 High Street, just above the Cheshire Cheese. He made and sold boots and shoes. James also had a similar shop at number 5 High Street. Later, his son John James did the same at 13 High Street.

James was married five times. One of his daughters was Annie Shaw who had Shaw's Iron Mongers. James' first son John James, married Frances Hobson from the Queens Head. They had four children John, George, Jessie and Lydia.

The Mottershead's were a very musical family. All six of them played the piano. Many evenings were spent singing in their home on 13 High Street. People would go stand in Wood's gennel to listen to them. John James and Frances Lydia used to sing duets at various concerts over many years.

John and George volunteered to join the forces at the outbreak of the First World War. John went into the Royal Flying Corps.

World War I fighter pilots had a typical life expectancy of just several weeks while flying in combat. In terms of flying hours, a combat pilot could count on 40 to 60 hours before being killed, at least in the early part of the war.

John James Mottershead. Phoenix Lodge of St. Ann No 1235. 1912.

George was in the trenches, including the battle of the Somme where he was wounded. I have the piece of shrapnel, which he said, saved his life, taking him away from the front line until he was fit again.

Richmond House. Can you spot the owner?

CORBAR HALL

Corbar Hall was built in 1852 as Corbar Villa for Blackburn brewer Henry Shaw. The architect was Henry Curry.

Picture taken from Kenny Robertson's facebook page.
Me and Mum, Daisy Pankhurst (bottom right in grey jumper) in Prima magazine back in... gulp... 1989!

Mum fought a campaign to keep Corbar Hall Maternity Unit (where yours truly was born) open for future generations, and won! I got a day off school to go and do this, so I was happy.

Facebook Posts

Jennifer Kelly

In Royal Blue uniform, Sister Rowlands, Black Jacket in the middle Margaret Mone, next to her back row Dr Geoffrey Willis, far right front row looks like Daisy Pankhurst, she delivered my first child. Can't remember the name of the lady with red hair but I'm sure it's not Maureen Trimmer. I think the other Doctor might be Brian Williams.

Diane Fletcher

Julie Lynall at the front. Diane Fletcher, Lynda McKernan back right. Looks like the amazing Dr Williams in the crease.

Shelagh Broadbent

Is that Dr Willis. I had 2 daughters there, I liked sister Mone.

Wendy Howe

Great days working there. I look back and feel very lucky to have worked with amazing and dedicated colleagues and to have the opportunity to be part of that team that provided a fabulous service to the community. Margaret Mone was my auntie and also my Godmother. She was a dedicated midwife who threw her life into Corbar. It was like a 5* hotel and I was very spoilt when I stayed there to have our sons Karl & Liam. I remember Joyce Stafford taking crying babies off to the 'Sin Bin' at night to allow the mum's to sleep. It's a crying shame it closed.

Jamie Stafford

Joyce was my Nan, I remember she rocked many a wee squealer back to sleep so their mothers could get some kip.

Heather Alcock

My beautiful mum worked at Corbar - Jenny Wright, she is still friends with Sue who also worked there. A lovely place and such a shame that we have no unit left now.

Karen Trimmer

Brilliant photo! Our mum Maureen Trimmer worked there in the 70s with her sister in law Margaret Mone.

Jane Bearder

Best place to ever have had babies... had both my girls there and every night they were taken into the nursery and fed by the midwives so mums could get plenty of sleep... if you wanted to feed your baby they would come and wake you and you'd go into the feeding room so as not to disturb anyone else... big shock when I had baby number three in hospital.

Hilary Nadin

Hotel Corbar. I went back to the Hall after my first child had to be born at Stepping Hill. A further three children were born at the 'new ' unit. Lovely, just lovely. Margaret Mone was on duty with the 4th birth, kept her on nimble toes as the birth was quick. Thanks to those lovely ladies.

Suzanne Beresford

Mrs Pankhurst delivered me in 1966 at Corbar and as a student nursery nurse I met her again on my three month placement there. The mums were so well looked after!

I wish I could have had my own children here!

Denese Pryce

I had my daughter Amy there, stayed ten days... just wonderful care. My son William was also born there, this time staying just a week. It was an amazing place, the care was excellent and I remember so many faces in the photo. Thanks for the memories.

Pauline Fletcher

Corbar was such an amazing place. Sister Rolands and Sister Mone delivered my first baby. Happy memories, the staff made you feel very special.

Dorothy Bonfield

I worked a bit of part time in the evenings with Miss Wagstaff and Miss Cooper, the cooks there in 1957, taking meals to the wards and helping generally. So it is good to read that Corbar Hall lasted for all those years. I still have my reference.

Alison Waterhouse

Wow, what a blast from the past! Had my daughter at Corbar Hall in 1986, the care was amazing, I was in for six days. I had a rubber ring to sit on and always remember Margaret Mone joking, she'd booked me a bed on the geriatric ward at the Cavendish.

Vicky Easton-Orr

I was born there! Not supposed to be but due to snow on the A6 and lack of time I was. Well done you, Mum!

Neil Bowers

First born Stepping Hill. Second two Corbar. Both places were tops. NHS at its best.

Mary Hibbert

My son was born there in 1976. The staff were wonderful.

Margot Graham

Both my children were born there. Such a loving atmosphere.

Jayne Thornton

In the early 70s when I had my three children, the Sisters and Midwives I recall were Smith, Downhill, and McDonald. Also I remember a small Irish lady who did the nightshift she was kind, funny and worked her socks off.

Sue Langley

I remember a little auxiliary nurse who was Irish, she would often say, 'Oh I do love the babbies!'

Wendy Lloyd

My mother May Gilbert was a midwife there in the 60s. Yes, the unit closed in 2012 at the Cottage Hospital but, as community midwives, we are still going strong and provide home birth service for our women in the High Peak.

Snippet

From 1956 to 1998 Corbar Hall was home to Buxton Maternity Unit.

In 2004 the unit was re-located to the Buxton Cottage Hospital and renamed Buxton Birth Centre. Alas in 2011, the NHS due to funding decided to close Buxton and Darley Dale units. Resulting in final closure July 2012.

c1984.

Infant and Child Welfare Centre, (off old Gas Yard, next door to 12A Bridge Street). The nurse in charge 1937 was Nurse A. Downes.

Jean Buckley

Jean Buckley recalls, as a pupil at Hardwick Square School, during the 2nd World War the school nurse would visit. We all dreaded it. She would check each child. A lot of us had a rash and been itching. When it came to my turn, alas she spotted a rash. This proceeded by me being taken by my mum, down to the child welfare clinic. The nurse examined me then proceeded to paint me from head to toe in lotion. I was then taken to stand in front of a big coal fire, while the lotion dried.

I can't remember what it was I had, I was only 6 or 7. Later the school nurse would be called the nit nurse by the children.

Ecton Picton and Margaret Hobson wedding photo, at Highfield 45 South Avenue.

Beth Jackson

George Hobson my Great, Great Grandfather was born in 1815. He left behind some very old parchment letters which I have in my possession. They are addressed to his son, also George, my Great Grandfather, who was born in 1846.

One of these letters, dated 1832, refers to him going to an auction in Alfreton with his brother in law Thomas Fidler.

Thomas bought the Queen's Head for £700-10-6d. He also bought the houses opposite the Queen's Head. These were known as Hobson's Court, for which he paid £27.

By 1847 the Duke of Devonshire was quoted as being Buxton's largest landowner. The remainder of the land was divided between seventy three people, four of whom owned the greatest amount, Great, Great Grandfather, George Hobson being one of them.

He built most of High Street as well as Torr Street, Bath Road and all of Rock Terrace. To this day I still receive chief rents for the latter two. Also built were the 14 houses on Mill Cliff, Silverlands.

"Freebody's Directory of Towns of Derby" 1852

Baker and Flour dealers.	George Hobson, Higher Buxton.
Cars and Phaetons.	Elizabeth Fidler.
Grocer and dealers in Sundries.	George Hobson, Higher Buxton. Market Place. (shop was established in the 1830s)

Taverns and Public Houses

The Queens Head. Higher Buxton.	Elizabeth Fidler.
The Swan. Higher Buxton.	W Fidler.
Museums, Market Place.	Samuel Fidler.
Sadlers. Higher Buxton.	Samuel Fidler.

Later the Queen's Head would be left to my Great, Great Grandfather, George Hobson by his mother-in-Law, Elizabeth Fidler. His son George (Grandad) would go on to own The New Inn Public House, also Hobson's Court on High Street and Hobson's Yard off Market Street.

In 1881, George Senior was 66 and living at The Queen's Head as Head Inn Keeper and Farmer of 17 acres.

Around the corner, at 14 Torr Street, George Junior was living. He was a Builder and employed 8 men.

It was rather strange that George Senior's son took over the Queen's Head as he was a Quaker, so was teetotal. He was the third generation to do so.

On Friday evenings, pay day, he would ask his customers to leave (if he thought they'd had too much to drink) and then he would take the rest of their wages home to their wives.

Family memories recall him standing at the doorway of the Queens Head throwing sovereigns to children and giving free drinks to passers-by. The Hobsons resided at the Queens Head for over half a century.

On leaving the Queens Head, certain artefacts were handed down through the family including a barometer which dates back to the 1830s.

Also a set of two tea-tables, one of which he decided to send to the Salerooms. However his Grand-daughter had other ideas, so she bought it back. These two tables are still in the possession of my sister and me, hopefully moving to my sister's two sons and onward.

Ian Howarth, The present owner of the "Queens Head" has two glass bottles on display which are inscribed, "Queens Head. G Hobson. Buxton".

Great grandfather George retired to Highfield, Hardwick Square on the corner of Darwin and South Avenues. The building was used by the Rechabites and is now four flats. Buxton Labour Exchange was built in the garden. That building is now occupied by Jehovah Witnesses.

One of the George Hobson's, not sure which, gave the first £50 towards the construction of the Town Hall clock tower, which cost £250 altogether.

Bill Hobson, my Grandma's brother emigrated to Canada before the first world war. On seeing the poster "Your Country Needs You" he decided to return back to England and serve his country.

Columbia Cottage.

Bill Hobson left. Dowlow Quarry.

When the War finished he returned home to Buxton. He built a log cabin, using logs sent from Canada, and called it Columbia Cottage. It was on the Ashbourne Road, near the "Bull-I'th'-Thorn Inn". The cottage was ideal, being within walking distance of his evening entertainment at the pub and his place of work, Dowlow Quarry. Here, he worked for my father Arthur Jackson.

The only descendants of the Hobson family still living in Buxton, apart from myself, are three grand-daughters of my great uncle Bill.

Betty Grable

Beth Jackson wearing her
Great Grandmother's wedding
dress. She is holding the Betty
Grable bag which she won in a
competition.

In the early 1940s Beth would walk home from Cavendish school with her friend Sylvia Dawson.

Their route took them via Terrace Road. On the fortnightly edition day of "Picturegoer", they would rush to Skidmore's Newsagents to buy a copy. It was in another newspaper, the Sunday Pictorial, along with 10,000 others, Beth entered a competition. To her surprise she came out winner of the Betty Grable bag which is still in her possession.

The lovely railings and gate long since gone for the war effort.

Kenneth Lees

I am a Buxtonian and proud of it. My life started in June 1940, not the best year to be born. Dad was already serving in the Army, on the top, of all places, Battersea Power Station, as an AA Gunner.

Growing up for me wasn't a problem really, nor was it for the rest of the kids on South Avenue. Oh, we knew things were hard without our dads about and with little money to buy food etc. My mum Betty worked long hours in a property on Fairfield Road for the Government forces engaged in decoding.

My Nan looked after me and our kid, my elder sister. Poor old devil she had her work cut out because she took in guests, mainly Operatics who were performing at the Buxton Opera House. Nan told us that our granddad had installed the electricity in the opera house years ago.

South Avenue was a lovely street and everyone did their best to keep it neat and tidy. Half the avenue was lined with Ash trees. My best mate Ronnie lived over the road from me in one of the six little whitewashed cottages, in a two up-two down, with a block of six outside toilets a good fifty feet across the backyard from the cottages.

Nobody ever seems to talk about the cottages nowadays, and I can't recall seeing any history on them, however there were some lovely families living in them, all of them treating us kids with kindness. They had lovely tended gardens leading to their front doors. More on them in a bit...

Our playground was the Pies, now Dale Side, especially around Mr Cliff Brunt's bake house. In later years, after the war, my dad used to work for him.

Our adventure ground was of course the cattle market... vastly different in those days. We used to scrounge rides on the horses and carts who kept the streets of Buxton spick and span. Later, when Buxton started to upgrade the local roads, there were large mountains of gravel chippings which to us was a fantasy land for Cowboys and Indians.

For entertainment we sometimes went to the Oddfellows Hall, up the rickety old stairs just on the right as you went in the door, which led to a large Hall. Local singers, many singing Vera Lynn, had us in raptures. Sometimes the old dears of the town held little tea parties (of course we weren't able to get a sniff of the goodies) followed by the inevitable 'Oldie Thyme Dancing'.

Back to the cattle market: If and when the great big cast-iron, orange pitch boilers were lit to melt the tar and, if any of us happened to have or had had colds we would be taken along by our folks. We were positioned close enough to inhale the fumes, which, by Jove, worked a treat in clearing up our germs in no time!

Every so often the local farmers would, with the help of their trusted sheepdogs, come from various parts of the outlaying farms with up to forty-odd sheep each to sell. I tell yer, them there dogs were fantastic, the way they kept the flock together with just a whistle from the farmers. Then they'd drive them into the pens which was a real treat for us youngsters! The big bonus for us 'Townies' of course was, as soon as the sales were over, out would come a dozen or so kids, with buckets, picking up the deposits the sheep left behind. Our hands were brown for weeks... but don't forget, it was our local allotment holders who supplied us with much of our veggies, spuds, cabbage, carrots, even garden peas. So a bit of sheep 'it' didn't harm us.

The corner of South Avenue and running across to South Street was a little hive of light industry, which added to the character of the place and we were more than happy to be raised in that part of Buxton.

"Who was who" on South Avenue and South Street? Well, in the Little Cottages were the Dawsons... Mum, Dad, (think he worked all his life in the Gas Works at the bottom of Dale Rd). The children, George, Evelyn,

Ronny and another brother. Then there were the Mitchells, another lovely family with Keith and Heather. (the reason I can't tell you Mum's and Dad's names is that we were told "It's Mr & Mrs to you kids" and that's the way it stayed... don't know if this is right but the saying went... "Manners maketh the child"). Then I think it was the Wells family and then the McKays and one 'Very Old Lady' at the end. We had Robinsons the window cleaners... the kids were Rex, Mervin, John, and Linda. Next door but one was the Needhams... later, some of them were to emigrate to Australia.

Our Most Famous Person on the Block was Sheila Blake at No 33 who, in 1946, was Buxton's Carnival Queen so all hands to the pump as they say. The residents begged, scrounged and delivered to decorate South Avenue and a real treat it looked.

Buxton was a lovely place to live although it showed the strains of WWII. We had a great deal of soldiers in town during the early 1940s, mainly from Canada and the USA. Most of them were in transit, leaving for war-torn Europe. How many of them never returned we would never know.

There were many Canadians who came back wounded and were cared for in the Devonshire Hospital, before being repatriated.

It was often said that during that time Buxton's birth rate increased considerably, also quite a few of our young ladies were to leave for pastures new in Canada and the USA.

Yvonne, I could go on, but fear I'd bore the pants off of you! Bear in mind I am no writer and I achieved One out of Ten for my, er... Academic Schooling!

Sheila Blake. Festival Queen 1946.

'THAT FOOD HALL LOCATION IS NO GOOD'

THE REC

1948 the Rec. My Gran, Charlotte Eyre and Mrs Wood. Both campaigners for preserving Cote Heath recreation area.

"Rec condition" Buxton Advertiser 1948

People living near the Cote Heath recreation ground have indignantly replied to Alderman J.W Wain's assertion to last week's meeting of the borough council that they were "unhelpful" and that the expenditure of putting the ground into reasonable condition was not justifiable in view of the public's attitude.

"It's all tosh!" declared Mr Nesbitt of Crowestones. "Of course people cut across the 'rec', when there are huge gaps in the hedges inviting them to do so. If suitable paths were made and asphalted, people would be only too delighted to keep to them. The trouble is that the Council is too lackadaisical about everything. They were a long time removing the emergency water tank and then they left a great yawning hole in the ground for months. If they had put a sandpit and even a paddling pool there it would have been a really good idea."

Remarks were "unwarranted" said Mr Eaton, of Bennett Street. "The work Alderman Wain spoke about was only half a job. As for the children carrying the stones about, they have to use them for wickets and you can't really expect them to put them back when they've finished. "The children wouldn't be half so destructive" added Mrs Eaton, "if there was more for them to play in, in the shape of a sandpit, a chute and roundabouts. Not that they are really destructive, they never go near the bowling green, or touch the flowers. Naturally they climb trees, what boy worth his salt wouldn't? But if they want to make Cote Heath into a park they will have to employ a park keeper".

Like many other residents, Mrs Sutcliffe of Byron Street was mystified. "The children play there," she said "but isn't that what it's for? I never see them doing anything wrong."

Mr H. C. Grimshaw of Sherwood Road, was emphatic: "It's silly to blame the people," he said. "The whole place needs going over. I've played football on that pitch, and I know it's dangerous. You risk a broken ankle every time you run."

Mr J Heywood of Newstead Terrace, expressed the opinion that "If anything like the care that is lavished on the Pavilion Gardens and Ashwood Park, was given to Cote Heath the residents would be delighted and have an incentive to keep the ground in good condition. If the council concreted the paths and planted a few shrubs it wouldn't go amiss. You can take it from me, we only use the footpaths in fine weather, as soon as it rains the place is a quagmire."

1950s-60s

Paul Booth

"The Rec" - Official name, Cote Heath Recreation Ground, surrounded by Byron Street, Kents Bank Road, Heath Grove (formerly called Recreation Road) and the rear of London Road.

If you look to the rear of the roads you will find evidence of many old stables. The Rec area would have no doubt been used for the many horses to exercise and graze.

When I was a child in the 1950s, the Rec playing area, was surrounded by hedges and gravel pathways, it consisted of two sets of swings, a seesaw and a twenty foot slide. It was an ideal spot to play.

From my own experiences it was a large part of my childhood. I and many of my friends spent most of our time there, the author of the book being one of them.

From dawn to dusk and sometimes, into the night, various activities would take place according to the weather and seasons.

SPRING AND SUMMER: Hailed such things as swing jumping, this consisting of jumping off the swings from a seated position. When you were as high as you dared, you would jump off, as far as possible (timing was important) onto a bare scattering of hay on a grassed base. I cannot recall anyone getting more than a cut knee... Amazing! (and swings were taller than they are today).

The slide, which was quite high, would be treated with candle wax and polished to a mirror finish making it extremely fast and slippery. Not only children partook to the slide. Fred Rancuch's dog was a regular user.

Talking of dogs, there was often stray dogs wandering around causing many of us to wonder why two dogs would get stuck together, back to back. Our parents would never tell us!

Dens would be built in the hedges. Holes would be dug as deep as we could, looking for treasure. When the grass was cut the hay could be blazed.

AUTUMN: The most important thing was the "Bonfire".

This was an enormous project, as was the finished bonfire.

It took many weeks to collect all the wood and other flammables and build it. The first items would be logs and branches. These would be collected from Grin Woods about a mile away up a steep hill. Around twenty boys and girls average age about ten and a couple of older boys would make at least three trips a day. Carrying them across a busy road, leaving a trail of broken twigs and leaves behind. The centre pole being the largest and the most important.

There were Sparklers, Jumping Jacks, Catherine Wheels, Roman Candles and Rockets to name but a few. Bangers were usually bought by the youth of the day.

WINTER: arrived and things got quiet, although the heavy snow falls gave us plenty of snow for igloos and giant snowmen as well as the customary snowball fights.

Rec kids include, Paul and Vicky Booth, David and Peter Thompson, Melanie Edge, Stuart Goodwin, Angela Wilkinson, the three Bradbury girls, Fred Rancuch, Dave Thomas, Derek Taylor, Peno Rossi, Murdo and Salti.

As we became a little older things changed. The council took much of the Rec for a school playing field. Of course we then reached puberty and the games changed somewhat. One thing that is still a mystery is why we hung around the public toilet at night. Strange!

Sadly, Paul died February 2018 and I am honoured to have this written work which he wrote September 2017. It's a cracker!

Snippet

Tom Markham, District Highways Superintendent, would, during Autumn, in order to save his workforce a job, instruct them that while pruning back the trees, not to load the cuttings and branches onto the removal van, but to leave them. They thought this rather strange. When they returned next day the cuttings and branches had disappeared.

The young bonfire collectors had been busy and bonfires in the area seemed to have doubled in width and height.

The Rec, 2017, on an autumnal Saturday afternoon. Shells of opened conkers lie in the damp grass amidst small wild mushrooms. There has been an abundance of growth, due to the exceptional summer. One spell was forty-eight days with no rain and near clear blue skies all the way.

The first person I come across is Jack Drogan, he's sat watching the football match. Jack's main reason for being at the Rec though is the skateboard and BMX enclosed area.

Steve Morten is stood a few metres away. He is supporting the Blazing Rag football team who are playing on the Kents Bank pitch. "The Rag" play in the Hope Valley A division league.

Whilst Steve is watching the game he keeps an eye on the busy play area particularly the rope swing where his small daughter is being happily pushed along, tended by a friend. It is half time, the Rag has just gone two- nil down. Oh dear.

As I leave I pass the enclosed, hard surfaced football and games area. At one half of the pitch round the nets, there is a group of eight or more special-needs young men. They are having a whale of a time. Two chaps are with them playing footie and apparently they go quite regularly. There is nobody using the Bowling Green today.

Round the corner stands the Blazing Rag (Manchester Arms) public house. Situated on one of the main roads into town, and close to residential housing, the pub has always maintained a regular clientele.

The original name for the public house was the Manchester Arms. 1908 / 1925, Kelly's Buxton directories show Thomas Hindle 'landlord'. A 1937 directory, Arthur Salt is at the helm.

When Michael McMahon first moved to Buxton, he took over the Clovercrest Cafe and Restaurant, 1 Market Place, on Valentines Day 1997. Not long after he was joined by Pauline.

On Valentine's day 1982, Michael and Pauline became landlord and landlady of the Prince of Wales public house, moving in with their three children.

A popular pub, built and owned by Mr Mycock in 1858. Well positioned at the bottom of Fairfield Road, the big hill and opposite Lightwood Road, plus Hogshaw.

The Prince was a good old nitty gritty proper public house.

When you were on a night out and entering through the Prince door it was with an element of the unexpected.

Barflys, workmen, regulars, darts, dominoes, pool players, bands, discos, jukebox, quizzes, birthday and other celebrations could be in full flow.

Michael was keen on football and was a member of the F. A. Council. The pub had its football team, yes, the Prince of Wales. Barry Nash a keen football fan and team manager was hands on. At that time there was the Taverners League and a couple of others.

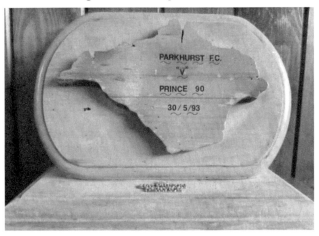

After matches the team would return to the Prince for sandwiches, food and a hopefully well earned drink.

Valentine's Day yet again, 1997, the McMahon's are on the move again, Proprietors at the Blazing Rag.

Michael Senior's passion for football continued as the successful team from the Prince followed him up to the Rag. Actually I think it was Pauline's sandwiches that did the trick! Over the years she dreads to think how many she made. Darts, dominoes, pool and football.

Pauline McMahon

Michael senior ran the Blazing Rag for 15 years. A good community pub with darts, dominoes, pool teams and plenty of characters.

Many of the young regulars ended up having families of their own, the next generation, clientele, and so on.

Michael junior took over from his dad in 2007 and bought his unique and popular touch to the pub.

Tradition carried on with lots of football, Michael being a Manchester City supporter, all good natured 'most of the time'.

Sadly Michael passed away but the spirit of Heath Grove and Buxton was amazing.

Snippet

The day of Michael's funeral, knowing there would be a large crowd paying their respects, Police cordoned off streets round St. Mary's Church.

I remember driving down London Road, everywhere I looked was a sea of "Men in Black".

THE STRICTLY COME DANCING SERIES HAVE BEEN SO SUCCESSFUL IN CHOOSING A WINNER THAT THIS METHOD OF SELECTION IS BEING CONSIDERED IN THE CHOICE OF OUR MP IN THE HIGH PEAK

HMS Vanguard.

Martin Turner

I was born at Corbar Hall in Buxton in 1975 to parents Suzanne and James (Jim) Turner. My first home was on Doveridge Grove in Fairfield. By the age of six my father's Painting and Decorating business was doing well so we moved to London Road. To me it was a huge new house and in fact was the tallest on the row.

My dad had set up his business with Colin Brace but, as partnerships tend to do, they eventually went their separate ways a couple of years later. A good number of the painters in this town learnt their trade at Turner and Brace, myself, Mark Waplington, Alan Ward, Colin Hall and Shaun Ennis to name a few.

Colin Hall often talks of the time back in the 1980s when he and my dad were doing a job painting off a very high ladder.

But the ladder didn't quite extend enough to reach the highest point of the building.

So Jim pulled his van right up to the house, stood the ladder on top of it and declared, "Get yourself up there Colin and don't take all day about it!"

Living on London Road meant that the 'Rec' behind us was basically our back garden and many hours were spent playing with other local lads such as Alan Wilson, Sean Beswick, Paul Dempster and Paul Scragg.

I particularly fondly remember Bonfire Night or Guy Fawkes Night. For weeks before, all the kids would knock on doors gathering everything and anything for the bonfire. One time the shop on the corner of London Road and Heath Park Road accidentally gave us a box full of menthol cigarettes. For the next few days every kid on the Rec became a smoker.

The council were our worst enemy as they didn't like us building our own bonfire. So when we were all at school they took it away. For the next couple of years the Manchester Arms pub {now the Blazing Rag} let us store our bonfire to the rear of the pub. They eventually withdrew their permission citing fire hazard as the reason but in truth they were tired of their back yard being a place where kids congregated.

Making a Guy was something that was done most years by me and my brothers.

We would collect 'Penny for the Guy' then with the money we would go down 'Boothies Gennel' to Mr Booth's which was a shop at the top of New Market Street and buy sweets.

One time a group of us local kids were on Byron Street and we didn't have the Guy with us. So we chucked someone, I forget who, into our wheelbarrow and tried our luck. The first homeowner wasn't buying our story and said he would put the Guy to the test. He went back into his house and came out with the biggest carving knife I'd ever seen. On sight of the knife the Guy was up and running for his life! You just can't pull out knives on children anymore... political correctness gone mad, ha ha!

I would still visit Fairfield often as my Grandparents, James and Alice Turner, lived up there. My Grandfather had been in the Navy a large part of his life. I only found out at his funeral that he had been torpedoed twice in WWII. Thankfully surviving unharmed both times. He continued in the Royal Navy on board HMS Vanguard. The Vanguard was the last ever battleship launched in the world at that time.

Whenever I visited him, to be fed and watered as he put it, he would still refer to things in the house as if he were still sailing the Seven seas. The kitchen was always 'The Galley' and he didn't just draw the curtains, he 'darkened ship'!

I now live in the same house he lived, with my wife Louise and children Max and Megan.

My daughter's bedroom is the same room my father grew up in. Whenever we close the curtains, we also say, 'Darken Ship'. It must work as the U Boats haven't got us yet.

DIY WAS NEVER MY STRONG POINT

COMPTON GROVE
FIRE STATION

Clive Upton

Compton Grove fire station came into being after the 1947 Fire Services Act. Until the start of World War II the fire service was provided by the local authority but in 1948 with the threat of war the auxiliary fire service was erected. Every borough and urban area had an A.F.S. unit of unpaid volunteers who operated parallel to the local authority.

In 1941 the local brigades and the A.F.S. were merged to form the National Fire Service. The 1947 act disbanded its N.F.S. and made fire fighting the responsibility of the county and county borough councils. The A.F.S. became a source to be used in the event of nuclear attack, using Green Goddess fire engines.

Two brigades were created by the 47 act in Derbyshire: the county and the county borough and these were continued until the local government reorganization of 1974 when the two were combined into a single brigade.

The fire station on Compton Grove was built and opened in 1952, its 6 bays and auxiliary building replacing existing buildings on Market Street (still there) and one on Palace Road (now demolished).

Buxton was also the Divisional Headquarters for B Division of

Derbyshire Fire Service with a total of 11 stations from Glossop in the north, Ashbourne in the south and the Hope Valley in the east. Buxton was the only all manned station in the division. Buxton provided a large amount of logistical support to the 3 day manned stations and the other retained stations. The amalgamation of the 2 brigades also led to the loss of Buxton control room when the system was centralised at Derby Head Quarters, Old Hall Littleover.

After reorganisation of 1974 its next big change came due to the 9 week national fire service strike 1977. This led to a change of hours and shifts resulting in a two-9 hour day and two-15 hour night shift and four days off, a reduction from 48 to 42 hours a week, it also created a 4 watch system of RED, WHITE, BLUE and GREEN.

The strikes resulted in a requirement for increased man power and this had Buxton being used as a training school; two of the houses the fire service owned on Compton Grove were used to house the recruits on the 3 month training course. If it snowed they had to clear the drill yard to enable training to continue. The last course finished at the end of May 1979.

At the beginning of the 1980's the houses, including divisional head quarters and the fire prevention offices were sold off and one bay of the main station was blocked up to allow accommodation for them on the 1st floor and create locker rooms thus displaced on the ground floor.

Training was ongoing, especially with an increase in more technical equipment across the years particularly in the area of Traffic Collisions. The development of larger H.G.Vs, more safety conscious cars all created their own problems, with more batteries, air bags, seat belt tensions, all causing potential hazards to the rescuers when involved in a collision.

R.T.C. (real time clock) were a major part of the work around Buxton and its Emergency Tender with heavier cutting equipment covering as far as Woodhead Pass. It didn't help that Buxton had officially some of the most dangerous road in the country in its turn out area.

Apart from fires and smoke alarms other regular call outs were for animals which had in all sorts off of ways got themselves stuck. These have covered everything from a duck stuck in mud in the Pavilion Gardens Lake to a very large Hereford Bull which had gone through ice on a pond, sheep on cliffs and cows stuck in slurry pits and a pony in a cattle grid. Children are quite good at getting stuck too, on the top of a red telephone box, up trees, and even on rides in the park.

Buxton always housed special appliances particularly a hydraulic platform and an emergency tender. These were often involved in different jobs including removing dangerous icicles from Buxton town centre. Away from the emergency call outs there were many other tasks that had to be carried out, maintenance and testing of equipment, inspections of premises under different acts, familiarisation of specific hazards in the turn out area, also more community work has become the norm, the home visit to fit fire alarms and give advice and talks to diverse groups and this area has been given increasing importance in recent times.

In 2009 the fire station on Compton Grove was replaced by a built for purpose greener building on Staden Lane and the old station and ancillary building were demolished and are now a housing estate.

Buxton Fire Station, Compton Road 2011. Courtesy of Graham Mitchell.

'DO EWE COME HERE OFTEN – OR ONLY ONCE?'

Arthur Jackson

Herbert William
Jackson

Beth Jackson

A rthur Henry Jackson, my grandfather, started "Dowlow Lime Stone Co. Ltd" in 1899. It was thought he was born before his time with many of his ideas, one being he thought powdered lime would be better than quick lime which was being used in the agricultural field. He tried to persuade farmers to no avail. In time Arthur was to be proven to be correct. Before and after his death he was often mentioned in the "Quarry Managers Journal". One such quote "A.H. Jackson had imported the first Symons crusher into England".

It was also quoted in a 1946 edition, "In the opinion of the associates engaged in the industry within the Buxton district, A.H. Jackson has without doubt, a far greater knowledge of the Limestone industry than any other man alive".

For over seventy years, seven members of my family were employed at Dowlow before it was sold to Steetley in 1969.

My father Arthur Jackson had 5 siblings Herbert, George, Winnie, Leslie and Bertha. He started work at Dowlow quarry on leaving school.

He volunteered to join the Army on the outbreak of the First World War in 1914 at the age of nineteen, in spite of being in a reserved occupation.

He served at Ypres and Loos, returning to Dowlow in 1919 spending the rest of his life there as Quarry Manager and Managing Director.

When his Father died in 1948 he became Chairman, until he died in 1966.

At the age of four, on his return from work, I would stand on the right hand side of the bridge to meet him off the 5.15pm train at Higher Buxton railway station, situated at the top of Peveril Road. Within a minute the platform went from being empty to being filled with one hundred and fifty men, having climbed from the fifteen train doors and its compartments. Dad was always in the middle of the crowd.

Beth Jackson would wait on the right hand steps waiting for her father.

Beth Jackson

Nobody else was being met, so I was a lone figure standing at the top of the long flight of wooden steps leading down to the platform.

Arthur's brother, Herbert William, was the Sales Director from 1934 and at one time held the title of President of the Institute of Quarrying. His other brother, Leslie was a Director and Secretary from 1940. Their sister, Winnie, was the Buxton office Manageress. My cousin Ian and sister Mary also worked in the offices at Buxton and Dowlow. The Buxton office was situated next to the railway station.

My father and uncle Herbert, together with Frank Anderson started the firm Equip Midlands Ltd in 1954. Frank also started the Lea Manufacturing Company of England Ltd. This was in collaboration with the Lea Manufacturing Company of Waterbury, Connecticut, USA. He also started the Eco Wheel Company Ltd and Lea Ronal (UK) Ltd, together these were known as the Anderson Group of Small Companies

Uncle Herbert was made a Justice of the Peace (Magistrates) on January 7th 1953 for the County of Derby until 1969, when he retired and went to Jersey.

He was Vice President of the Derbyshire branch of "The Institute of Quarrying" in 1953 and he was President of "The Limestone Federation". Always a keen golfer he was Captain of the High Peak Golf Club 1942/43.

When my Father died in 1966 Herbert became the managing director and chairman until he retired in 1969.

Dowlow was taken over by Steetley, then Redland, Lafarge, Hope and now Breedon. One company for 70 years then five companies in 49 years!

The company produces the purist limestone in the country, so pure it is an essential ingredient of the glass bottle trade, and supplied direct to the food industry. Sales from the quarry equal about ten million tonnes a year.

Dowlow produces twenty two products, some of which are blended to make a sale list of around forty products. Twenty percent is sold into the industrial markets and eighty percent to the construction markets.

Most Dowlow employees live within a ten mile radius, hence contributing to the local community and economy.

LIFE ON THE ROAD

Keith Wood

Keith Wood arrived in Buxton from Marple, seeking work, aged 22, it was 1971. The Quarrying industry was thriving.

Dowlow, Eldon Hill, Ashwood Dale, ICI Tunstead, ICI Hindlow, Topley Pike, Hill Head, Ryan and Somerville, Beswick's, Hughes Bros (Waterswallows) and Grin Quarry were all in operation at this time.

Blasting time at Grin Quarry: It had been known that, if the potent mix of dynamite was not quite correct, Burbage residents would be the victim of rocks and debris, which would scatter, landing on roads, gardens and yards, much to their annoyance.

Meanwhile, down on the A6, below the Ashwood Dale Quarry, two men would go to stand. They would have two flags, listen for the warning sirens and halt oncoming traffic in the vicinity. When the all clear sounded, traffic proceeded as normal.

Quarry faces would be plugged with dynamite, the fallen limestone rock, would then be transferred to the processing plant. Here, the limestone would be crushed to various specifications and processed accordingly to the needs of the customer.

The haulage driver would arrive early in the morning, load up, drive onto the weighbridge and off to his destination. During summer the haulage driver's loads were usually for roads and houses. Winter would be factories, sugar beet etc.

After a year living and working in Buxton, Keith managed to buy his own lorry an old "Commer" for £450.

One of his first trips in his "Commer" was taking a load of lime from Beswick's Quarry. The order's address was; Water Treatment Plant, Sherlock Road, Reading.

Briggs sidings. Hindlow Quarry in background.

A later job was delivering materials to Hindlow Quarry for the laying of Hindlow railway sidings. The materials would have to be picked up at ICI Tunstead sidings. Henry Boot was the contractor and Ashton Vernon Aggregates, Macclesfield were his supplier.

Ironically a local supplier could have been used, cutting out the despatching from Ashton Vernon to Tunstead.

From experience, up till the demise of the Tarmac fleet, there was much camaraderie amongst the men and to a degree, management. We would all watch out for each other, complete a good day's work, using our own initiative without much hassle.

This would change around 1992, with the birth of the "Tarmac owner driver".

The job became much more serious, to the detriment of the established work force. Alas, the upsetting of the apple cart was looming, the cost of fuel, satellite plants and major cities having their stone brought in by rail. The outcome was haulage work reduced in the area, never really coming back, not like it used to be. We had to digress, look for other jobs.

A group of lorry drivers laid off because of the recession met for a social at Fairfield Liberal Club to mark the end of an era.
The drivers were formerly employed by Tarmac and they made up the North West fleet based at Topley Pike and Waterswallows quarries. Between them, the drivers had given over 700 years service to the firm.

Peter Blanco

Once, at the top of Upper Hulme hill, fully loaded ERF artic, I changed down a gear, because it's one hell of a steep hill. As it went into neutral the gear linkage broke. So, I let it free wheel down... no use using your brakes because they would fade. I ended up across from that lay-by with the phone box, near the army barracks.

I lit a fag, rang Sam Longson's or it may have been Hanson's, to come and sort it. It was a nasty one but I walked away without a scratch.

I was working for "unnamed". It was a Volvo F12 artic tipper again. I was told to bring my truck in for new brake linings all round and my trailer on Friday, and to pick it up early Saturday morning.

My job was to pick up two loads out of Dove (Holes) and deliver, I think it was to Sandbach. Anyway, because I had new brakes and two loads, I went the quickest route which was up the Cat and Fiddle, turn left for Congleton and over what they call the Dumbers. I was right near the bottom when I had no brakes whatsoever... I even pulled the park brake and the pull button (dead man switch). Still nothing and we are speeding up and it's happening really quick. You have milli-seconds to act. On my left was a wall about 2ft high with a drop, on my right was an embankment and a big tree. I through it up the bank so as to just miss the tree and over she rolled, fully loaded with lime. Well I hung on, expecting everything to go black. Yep, everything was in slow motion, or, your brains taking in so much it feels that way. It's a narrow road so my cab was getting crushed on the passenger side, sliding down the road. Hot oil was coming out of the engine, I felt it behind me, the windscreen blows out and, "Pete me owd lad, this is it"! I thought.

Then the sounds all stopped, the truck had stopped and I was still sat in an upright position frozen stuck to the steering wheel. I climbed out of the door like it was a tank. I stood on top punching the air, shouting all sorts and not a scratch on me! As I was shouting my appraisals out, a white artic came around the corner with a kid in the passenger seat who looked no more than twelve. The corner was a left hooker, I wouldn't have made.

I would have ended up in the reservoir or a head on with the white artic that was a left.

The police came. The guy who owned the house nearby thanked me for dropping limestone on his garden, and brought me a cup of tea. He was right chuffed!

Anyway, the police kept on and on and on asking me was I ok. "Yes" I said. "Are you sure?" "Yes" I said. "Are you completely sure?" "YES!" I yelled. "No need for that... calm down." the policeman said, winding me up even more. Anyway, the wrecker came and before they could put it back on its wheels they would have to wind the brakes on manually.

While they were doing the brakes, my boss Stan arrived, mouthing it off. The wrecker guy shouted over that there were no brakes left. I said "It had new linings on yesterday". "Nope" he said. "No new brakes here. I bet your man just wound them up".

By now I was seeing red so I picked up my shovel and chased him up the hill. I was just about to strike when this copper grabbed me and pulled me back. He got in his Landrover and drove off. The road was closed for 8 hours due to power, phone lines, repair and recovery.

'THEY SHOULD PROVIDE A COLOUR CODED REFUSE BIN FOR FAG ENDS'

Blue Bird. Creating the world's land speed record. Duron Brake Linings Ltd, Buxton, Derbyshire.

DURON BRAKE LININGS

Roy Booth

Duron Brake Linings Company was founded by Alfred Bailey on the 19th Dec 1927. He had been a Captain with the Royal Engineers during the First World War and whilst on leave in 1917, he met Herbert Frood's daughter Millicent, whom he later married. They had two children, Peter and Pat.

After Alfred's release from the army in 1919, Herbert, the founder of Ferodo Ltd, offered him the job of Works Manager at his factory, in Chapel-en-le-Frith. During 1925 Ferodo Ltd was sold to Turner & Newall Ltd. Alfred then decided to start up his own company in Buxton around Bridge Street. Sometime later Alfred was joined by John Atkinson, an industrial chemist. Together they further developed the manufacturing processes for making friction materials.

Following Alfred's death in 1952, Peter took over the firm but sadly he died shortly after, at the early age of 39. His sister Pat (then Mrs Riley) took on the role of Chairman. Pat died in 2008.

The company brand name DURON, was created in the early period of opening. It was derived from the Latin word 'durare' (hard wearing).

Under the DURON brand name the company gained steady success during the 1930s and 40s. Linings were fitted to motorcycles at the early Isle of Man TT races and were famously used by Sir Malcolm Campbell, on his world speed record breaking Bluebird car.

The original Duron factory was built on the old town gasworks. The sunken bases for the gasometer were used to house resin dipping tanks for woven cloth, in what was known as the Process room. It is thought that the site once included a Bake house. The office block, fronting onto Bridge Street, originally belonged to the IXL laundry, which had moved to new premises further along Bridge Street. A new fabricated building was constructed in 1953/55 at the rear of the site.

Around the year 1948, a row of houses and outbuildings known as Brittain's Buildings, Wye Street, had been purchased and was used for office space, finished stores, canteen and the drilling and reline departments. These buildings were situated on the other side of the adjacent river Wye and were connected to the main site by a couple of footbridges.

Peripheral Buxton sites once used by Brake Linings Ltd.

Nunsfield Road. Up to the early 50s the dry mixing plant and joiners shop were sited in two storey buildings half way up.

Shakespeare Garage, Spring Gardens. The first floor of this building was used to house and maintain the company vehicles.

Charles Street. In the late 1950s, B.L. Ltd vacated Shakespeare Garage and took over the old North western Bus Company premises along with an adjacent building owned by the CO-OP. Up until the early 60s the site, now Buxton Building Supplies, was used as a garage facility for making disc pads and the refurbishing /relining of brake shoes.

Stud Riding School. Waterswallows Road. From the late 1950s this quite large building, no longer there, was used as a storage depot for raw materials until the 1960s.

Stowtime Ltd, Harpur Hill, (previously the Mushroom factory). After vacating the Waterwallows site, raw materials were housed in a couple of large underground bays at Stowtime. These were part of the extensive system of war-time tunnels.

Spring Gardens. Suite of offices above what is now Ponden Mill, housed the Purchase and Export departments.

Beanstocks, (former knitting factory off Queens Road Fairfield). Now the site of a Housing Close. Used for Finished Stores and Despatch, moving up to Ashbourne Road.

In 1964 a new building was erected on the site of the old Bridge Street Clinic, allowing the vacation of the Nunsfield Road site.

By this time it was realised that further expansion of the Bridge Street Factory was impossible so it was decided to move to a new out of town site.

Luckily the Bailey family had anticipated this, and, in 1952 had bought a 12 acre plot of land, off the Ashbourne Road at the junction with Staden Lane.

Construction duly followed and the 1960s saw the construction of a new purpose built factory.

By the mid-seventies, Duron was a successful company with a deservedly large share for truck, bus and industrial products but the threat of Asbestos being banned on health ground was ominous. Faced with the prospect of huge class actions from the USA, during the mid-1980s Asbestos was finally banned. The Directors knew that we didn't have the technical resources to re-invent our products without the basic raw material.

This was the background to the company being taken over by T&N. Sadly the ban caused serious financial problems leading to the eventual collapse of T&N worldwide and the total reorganization of the Ferodo division.

By 1983 the move was completed after a slow and gradual removal of all machinery, equipment and staff. The old Bridge Street factory was demolished making way for the Spring Gardens relief road, car parks and the new shopping centre.

The new factory on Ashbourne Road became extremely busy, with three shift working in most sections and, at its peak, employed over 500 people.

With the introduction of automation to the press lines, production exceeded well over a million brake linings per year.

Soon after the move, the company was sold to T&N Ltd who placed it under the wing of the Ferodo board. Production continued and proved to be a good fit with the Ferodo range.

However in 1996, Ferodo Ltd was bought out by the American company Federal Mogul Corporation. Sadly, this eventually resulted in the Buxton site, with all production, being transferred to other factories across Europe.

Robbie Jones

I started work at Duron's Ashbourne Road site in November 1975. The shift was between 6pm and 10pm, hence the Twilight Shift title and consisted wholly of women. The work was hard, hand-blistering, unbelievably foul smelling, dirty and tedious. We stood at various machines, drilling, stencilling and chamfering individual brake slabs then stacking them into wheeled trolleys.

We worked a four hour shift, Monday to Thursday for the princely sum of around £11 per week – a good sum then. Equal pay for women wasn't implemented here until 1978 although the act passed in 1974.

A transport van was provided from the Bridge St. factory to the Ashbourne Rd site and driven by Billy Downings. The van had wooden benches on either side of the inside space with not a seat belt in sight. Today's Health and Safety brigade would have a fit. Names I remember on the Twilight Shift:

Names I remember:

Barbara Bateman, Judy Beadman, Shirley Hunt, Sue Wilson, Mick Fletcher, Anne Welby, Chris Hindle, Kathy Morson, Pat Goodwin.

Supervisors: Stan Gill, Harold Scragg, Pete Bell, Derek Fletcher, Bill Boulton, George Barber, Ron Foxton, Dennis Gilman... all characters in their own way.

Stan Gill had been a submariner in WWII and told harrowing tales of days on end, submerged under the Skaggerrak Strait in Scandinavia.

Harold Scragg had been a marine and this showed. He ruled with a rod of iron... literally! If anyone stepped out of line on his shift, they knew it... the iron rod came into use! No-one complained, it was how it was in the 70s... and Harold really was a lovely guy!

Ron Foxton was a character in his own right... always smiling, ready with a joke at all times but fair and helpful... a thoroughly nice bloke.

The presses were manned by teams of men making the brake linings. (Much harder than the finishing work that we women did). Brake lining mix was weighed and tipped into the heavy metal dies then pushed along rollers into the presses to be compacted by hydraulic weights. All manual, heavy work... automation was a long way off. It was strenuous, unbelievably dusty, smelly, hot and mind-blowingly boring work. In Summer the heat and smell from the presses was unbearable, how the men endured it I don't know, they worked continually bathed in sweat, they were a hardy lot. There was always an air of camaraderie though and everyone just got on with the job – mostly good natured. And regardless of weather, people got to work. There was a "get up and deal with it" attitude then. One particularly hard winter, with huge snow drifts blocking roads in and out of Buxton, one of the day workers, Brian 'Tiger' Grimshaw, fought his way through knee/ waist high snow from Longnor- 4 miles out of Buxton to clock on. (just to say he couldn't work due to the weather!). then fought his way back through the snow to Longnor. It must have taken him hours! But if you failed to turn in, you didn't get paid: Simple. And he wouldn't have had a phone in his house so had to make the trek.

Heavy, long lasting snow was the norm in Buxton then and people just dealt with it, got on with it and did what had to be done. It was how it was.

Another anecdote: One of the pressmen, Monty Bellfield, had a side-line smallholding with a few 'beasts' (cows) which needed transferring from one side of town to the other, He enlisted the help of some of his fellow press-men who had completed their shift quota early. They drove this small herd of beasts through the main streets of town in the early hours of morning. They had to pass White Knowle Road where one of the site managers, Bill Ward, lived. Some of the beasts chose that precise moment to break away and they clattered down past Bill's house with the lads in frantic hot pursuit to bring them back to the herd.

Had they been discovered there may have been severe repercussions! There was a far more easy-going attitude in those days, a blind eye was turned to various activities within the factory, but this escapade may have been considered a step too far had it come to light.

Asbourne Road Managers

Roy Booth. An accomplished artist. He had a huge oil painting of a steam engine behind his desk.

Bill Ward, Barry Crawford, Ian Patterson, Brian Dobson, Derek Lindley, Tommy Woods, Norman Eyre and more whose names I forget. I'm not sure of the titles of the above.

Shop Floor Pressmen

Dave Buxton (Bucko or Manny), John Calladine (Cal), Geoff Hodgkinson (Oggy), Monty Bellfield, Cliff Bellfield, Mick Brooke, Steve Armitt (Herman), Peter Armitt (Joss), Trevor Andow, Sid Banks, (wife Christine in offices), Raoul Bolton and many more, again, I forget names.

Mixing Room

Dave Cooper, Steve Harrison, Melvyn Walton, Simon Jones, Chris?

Finishing Dept.

Yvonne Connick, Jean Kelly, Greta Owens, Doreen Barler, Nellie Morrison, Doreen Bradbury, Mary Gregory, Kath Turner, Margaret and Dave Wardle, Terry Fletcher and many more.

Finished Stores

Janet and Tony Woolford, Gwen Swindells, Kurt Bolton, Arthur Sutton

Laboratory and Lab Offices

John Gilman, Mike Hibbert, Terry Pheasey, Paul O' Hanlon, Peter Clayton, Mary Pimblett, Dave Critchlow (Bunk), Robbie Buxton, Ken Oliver, George Barber, Jock Wood, Wendy Woods, Jayne Taylor, Carole Wall, Chrissie Redfern, Julia Berrick, Alison and Chris (?), Peter Denton, Dave Polykett.

The canteen was brilliant, run by Les Gordon, Phyllis Murfin and Gwen Bagshaw. Phyllis was a great cook, her Cheese and Onion Pie was legendary as was the Thursday Roast Pork Dinner. A real treat for morning break on Thursday was pork dripping, straight from the Roast Pork tin and smothered on toast. Such a healthy snack... and we all queued up for it and loved it!!!

Steve 'Ammo' Hampson was in the Engineering Stores and recently told the story of the amazing generosity of Duron folk, when he tragically lost his partner after the birth of their daughter. He is still amazed and grateful for the friendship and support he received. A collection was organised by the ladies on the shop floor and £1200 was raised and shared between Ammo and a fellow worker, who had also suffered tragedy. This was a huge amount to be raised in the early 1980s. Another collection produced new and used baby items - it took Ammo a fair while to suss out how a baby gro went on! The ladies also knitted clothes for his tiny daughter... such was the sense of camaraderie among the fabulous people of Duron.

John Limer was the firm's Garage Mechanic, keeping the fleet of wagons roadworthy. A gentle giant of a man, he was an important cog in Duron's chain. At a time when winter meant regular heavy falls of snow, John and his mate (can't remember his name) kept the Ashbourne Road clear for traffic so that we workers and suppliers could get to Duron. At that time of severe winters, all industry in this area, including the quarries, kept snow-clearing equipment as a matter of course, to keep the roads clear, so that business could continue as usual. Not so these days!

I moved from the Twilight Shift onto the full-time Day Shift around '78 and then into the Laboratory where I remained until '98 and can honestly say that it was a real 'family' place to work in.

Duron employed over 500 people in its heyday, so contributing to the wealth and wellbeing of the town for several decades. Conditions were pretty good albeit with very hard physical work for some.

There was a social club which most people joined for a minimal weekly sum. Benefits included arranged outings, Christmas parties for retired workers and for children of workers. There were regular meetings, sports days and tournaments including Darts and Dominoes, which anyone could partake in. There were several social gatherings throughout the year which were always well attended and they were always enjoyable.

The company implemented a health scheme with dental and optical benefits, payments for hospital stays etc., and they introduced a Pension Scheme, the company matching employees' contributions. I think it can be safely said that Duron took care of its workers.

Duron was absorbed into its sister company, Ferodo (now Federal Mogul), in March, 1999.

Snippet from the Author

Monty Belfield also had another side-line on his smallholding. Turkeys raised specifically for the Christmas Day dinner table. His work mates usually lent a hand, plucking the turkeys in Monty's front room... Monty's poor wife Anne, was very long-suffering! I personally remember receiving one said turkey as its skin had been slightly torn so was not sellable. It was huge and filled every corner of the oven... Monty didn't do small or medium!

Brenda Hilton

Memories of Buxton. Most of my class left school in 1964-65 and started work straight away at Coopers "the corset factory". It was a factory in the woods across from the Blazing Rag. We started by learning to thread the industrial machine up to speed, as we would be doing piece work. Next we learned to sew straight lines on paper. Once we were able to keep it on the lines we then tried it on bits of material. After six weeks of training they gave us some work to do.

Once on the shop floor we joined the rest of the sewers on a line. Soon enough I was sewing pretty well and was put on 'Panties and Roll-ons'. After a while they shifted us around so we learned more about the different pieces that made up a Bra or Roll-on.

My first weeks wage in late 1964 was £4 19s 99p. (one penny off a fiver). I thought it was good, so we went out to see groups at the Pavilion Gardens at ten shillings (50p) to go in. The Who, The Kinks, The Hollies and P. J. Proby all appeared there. I loved the groups on a Saturday night!

Then it was back at work on Mondays. In the factory they had a record player and they would use the tannoy so we could sing along as we sewed.

A few years on I left and joined a mad crowd of girls picking mushrooms at the Mushy Farm as we called it. We worked hard for our money. There was some ladies working there who would nick our mushrooms if you weren't quick, though there was always plenty.

I helped out with the watering of the mushrooms, it was a change. We had fun with Keith Howard. I had to fill a large tank with water and put chloride in it to lighten the mushrooms and kill any bugs. Well, one day, as Keith went past me I wet him just a bit. So he lifted me up and dumped me in the tank! I was wet through but it didn't matter... we were young and having fun. After a while a new boss came and changed all the way we worked. He was American. Not long after, there was a blight of bugs and red mites all over everything so it closed down.

So, back to the corset factory. By then it was making lovely lacy bras and panties to match. I made a load of money! I got married in early 1972.

Early 1980s.

RAF HARPUR HILL

Bill Grant was a young man from Scotland, stationed in the RAF at Harpur Hill. After the war, Bill and his two friends (fellow Scotsmen) remained and made their homes in Buxton.

One of the reasons that swayed them was having met three Buxton ladies. Ironically, the three were all employed by Churchill's hairdressers situated on Station Approach.

The blushing brides were: Alma Taylor who tied the knot with Ian Morin, Beryl Fletcher who married John Copstake and Bill (Jock) Grant getting hitched to Mavis Dean.

Snippet

I guess the lads all got free haircuts whilst they were courting! The RAF left in 1960.

RAF Harpur Hill was originally an ammunitions dump, it opened in 1938 and closed in 1960. It was once the biggest ammo dump in the country, over 500 acres. 11 rail tunnels and an underground store were cut deep into the countryside.

Gas weapons and V bombs were stored here amongst other things.

The RAF also had UXO units (bomb disposal) based here and later, Mountain Rescue teams.

In 1961, following the departure of the Air Ministry in 1960, an auction was held by Hampson's to sell houses which had been built for the RAF personnel and families. Harris Road, Tedder Avenue, Kedleston Avenue, Nettleton Lane and Trenchard Drive were not mentioned in that particular sale article.

Possible origin of the above road names:

Harris Road:

1st Baron, Air Marshal Arthur Travers Harris (1892-1984) GCB. OBE. AFC.

He was commonly known as Bomber Harris but also, in the mess room, as Butcher Harris. Arthur served in the first and second World Wars. Including the 2nd World War, Arthur's years of service amounted to thirty two years. He achieved the rank of Marshal of the Air Force.

Tedder Avenue:

1st Baron, Air Marshal Arthur William Tedder (1890 1967).

Arthur started his military career in the Army until he was wounded in the knee. He then changed course and joined the RAF in 1916. Until the end of the War he served as pilot and squadron leader, seeing action on the Western Front. His bombing tactics became known as the Tedder Carpet. During the 2nd World War he was with the Air Ministry as Director General of research and development.

He was also present at the signing of 'The German Instrument of Surrender' in Berlin 1945.

Nettleton Road:

John Dering Nettleton VC. (1917-1943)

Although born in Nongoma, Natal Province, South Africa his allegiance was with the United Kingdom.

He was commissioned with the Royal Air Force in December 1938. By 1940 he had been promoted to Flying Officer. In February 1941 he became Flight Lieutenant and was a squadron leader. Nettleton was awarded the Victoria Cross for his part in an air mission involving two formations of 6 heavy Lancaster bombers over Augsburg, Germany.

In July 1943, he was on a flying mission to Italy which numbered 295

Lancaster's. Returning home his group of Lancasters were attacked over the Bay of Biscay. Nettleton and his crew were among the losses. Their bodies were never recovered.

Trenchard Drive:

Hugh Montague Trenchard 1873-1956. Marshal of the Air Force, 1st Viscount Trenchard GCB, OM, GCVO, DSO. He was a British Officer and Air Marshal who helped lay foundations of the Royal Air Force (RAF).

As a boy he struggled academically and only just met the requirements for him to be commissioned into the Army. Whilst in the Army he fought in the Boer War in South Africa. Here he was critically wounded, resulting in the loss of a lung and being partially paralysed. To recuperate he travelled to Switzerland. Whilst bob-sleighing there he had a heavy crash. After the accident, Trenchard found that his paralysis had gone and he was able to walk unaided and able to continue his career in The Army.

After being invalided home in 1912 he learned to fly, and in 1913 became Assistant Commander of the Central Flying School. 1915 he took command in the Royal Flying Corps, a branch of the British Army. His policy of launching persistent attacks in order to establish dominance of the air became the standard doctrine of Britain's Air Force.

In 1930 when he had retired from the Military, Hugh took the job of Metropolitan Police Commissioner.

Kedleston Road:

Possible link to George Nathaniel Curzon, 1st Marquis of Kedleston Hall and President of the Air Board.

Wrington Vale Mushroom Farm

Charlie Clark- Driver

In 1964, after lying empty and neglected, the tunnels had a new lease of life, becoming Wrington Vale Mushroom Farm. At the time it was the world's biggest mushroom producer. In the first few months of production, 2,000lbs of mushrooms were being produced at the site, with 5 times that amount by the end of the year.

Facebook comments

Kenneth Lees

It was owned by Graham Griffiths & Jonathan Shaw, who had a much smaller farm in Somerset. Pat Martin was general foreman and carried out most of the setting up work, he was a great guy.

Dave Hollins

Haha, I worked at the Mushy. I was one of the tunnel tractor drivers, along with John Gould and Barry Wilmot. Nigel Wilson and Stewart Twigg were the tunnel fork lift operators. Pelli and Pete Stableford did the house cleaning. There are lots more to name of the people that worked there. Correct me if I'm wrong but I do believe that.

Unfortunately, the mushrooms got a bacteria that they couldn't control and the mushroom factory was closed.

Jacqueline O'Meara

My dad used to drive a mini bus full of workers to and from the mushroom factory. I love mushrooms!

Gary Nadin

My dad drove the buses, also one of the wagons with Sam Salt. I used to go with him to the stables to pick up the horse muck. Good times.

Brenda Hilton

I worked there when it was the mushroom farm in 1966, at weekends and school holidays, fun times. Eileen Cornwell was there and Keith Howard was head of watering, which I worked on.

Denyse Hall

I worked there in the holidays and at weekends too! It paid good money if I remember correctly.

Carol Cotterill Mellor

I used to go to help mum on a Saturday.

Christine Gormally

I worked there on a Saturday and holidays. Got up at the crack of dawn, picked up a basket, a lamp and knife and went down the tunnel. A bit scary in the dark.

Bill Sandeman

I always peel my mushrooms because I remember all the rats in those tunnels.

Izzy Hertzog

I went to the mushy farm nursery while my mum picked mushrooms!

Gwen Hicken

Liz Nash

I worked at the Mushroom farm when I was 16. It was a rare job and a bit scary too. Dad was manager there until the day it closed. I feel the urge to write about my time working there, it was such a presence in my teenage years and for my family.

Karen Munro

I worked picking mushrooms, it kept you fit climbing up and down the beds and I enjoyed every minute. I also entered the mushroom Queen contest.

Corrida Kersey

My mum, Trenna Turner worked there when I went to school in the old school house, Harpur Hill.

Beryl Limer

Best job ever, picked many mushrooms, happy days! Met hubby (John) there he worked in the garage. Good fun x

Mary Bronzo

So did I. What a stink !!!

George Chalkley

My mum and dad worked at the mushy farm and that is how they first met.

Margaret Bingham

12 pound a week I got. Gil Bingham worked there in 1975 for 6 months. My cousin Len Alsop was a Foreman.

Cheryl Wagstaffe

I worked at the mushy factory when the kids were little - great days - sometimes the electricity would go and we'd be plunged into blackness - really eerie!

Jon Davies

My mum Nancy Davies used to work in there picking.

Vicky Easton-Orr

My Mum & Dad both worked there! Pam Clark worked there too xx

Rob Wagstaffe

£5 for a Saturday morning shit shovelling in 1965. Beer was 1/8d a pint (8p). Happy days, and some great guys to work with!!

Denise Wood

Me and my mum used to work there. My Mum was Jean Dobson.

Tanice Pickford

My Dad drove the loco's loaded with ammo during the war and my Mum was canteen manageress there when it was the mushy farm.

Valerie Brindley

My dad used to be a foreman up there. I remember going to one of the Christmas parties for kids.

Carol Cotterill

My mum worked there as well as at Duron Brake Linings.

Anne Needham

My mum Margaret Wilkinson worked there during the war when the tunnels were full of bombs etc!

Larry Zamirski

I worked there when it was Stowtime in the late 70s... good days really... even though there was a recession etc.

Agnes Hamill

I and three other ladies from Ireland worked there in the late sixties. We stayed in a Hostel that was part of the factory.

Stephen Shibby Hibbert

John Copstick, who I worked with at Buxton Fire Station, came to Buxton when he worked at Harpur Hill. It was an RAF station and he stayed here. He was a great bloke.

John O'Meara

I had to go and do a job every Friday afternoon in the Packing Room! Also a regular job, starting at 06:00 Saturday mornings in the manure shed!

Anne Baker

Did a bit of part-time work there at week-ends.

Denny Holland

I worked there for two weeks. Put me off mushrooms for life.

Sue Balfe

Yes Tracey, I worked every Saturday with all the Italians in Buxton. We had great fun and Aunty Madge was a supervisor. The lift would get stuck going into the tunnels and it was scary but it was great fun x

Linda Hunt

I worked there in the holidays. I was Linda Syrnicki then.

Pelle Gaglione

I used to work There!

Geoff Clark

I worked at the Mushy. Dad was transport manager, Mum ran canteen.

James King

I worked up there for a short time. It was very bizarre place... you could really sense the history!

Paul Goodwin

School holidays and weekend work picking mushrooms. Good money but a horrible job!

Kevin Hen

Great money if you like the smell of mushrooms.

Kat Louise Paterson

My family worked there.

Bev Jane

My mum worked there too x.

Liz Prentice Hunter

I worked there. It was good money and great fun.

Jeanette Ball

Picked many a mushroom there... lol.

Modfather Baldy

Worked there in the 70s.

Jeanette Kelly

I think we all worked there over the years ,my mum was one of longest there till it closed. When I worked at Stowtime years ago, they took us down into the tunnels, felt very strange x.

Geoff Kidd

Worked there Richard from 1970 until it closed in July 1976.

Dave Hollins

I have to say Gwen was a good boss.

Jayne Cocker

It was the awful smell on you when you came home.

Steve Prime

I used to work in the mushroom farm c1965.

Gillian Zoppi

My mum worked there too.

Neville Higton

Worked there for twelve years.

Brenda Hill

I worked there at weekends when I was a teenager.

Keith Sandy

Bin boy on a sat morning when I was 14.

David Critchlow

Hated it there. Poor money, too dark and my boss was a ----- .

Jane Barson

On a Saturday when I was a teenager in the 70s, some of the tunnels were said to be haunted. My Grandad drove a forklift there for a while and he said he saw a ghost one New Year's Eve! He had an accident and broke his arm as a result of it!

John Barry East

My Grandad worked there in the 50s when it was the Air Ministry.

Rick E Pinder

I worked there, Christian Salvasson.

Jon Davies

I worked in there when it was Stowtime, packing cheese.

Helen Paula Salt

I worked there at Salvenson Stowtime.

Amanda Mycock

I worked there at Norbert Dentressangle.

Mushrooms!

IT'S RUMOURED THAT NEXT YEAR'S DANCING ON ICE WILL BE BROADCAST FROM BUXTON FOOT PATHS

ENTERTAINMENT

Buxton throughout the generations, as a place of its size, always had an abundance of musicians and artistes of all genres. Not just in theatres, but church and congregational halls, public houses, clubs and even street corners.

In 1903 Buxton Opera House opened, bringing the whole spectrum of entertainment to our doorstep. Ballet, Opera, Drama, Shakespeare, Music, Cinema, Comedy... you name it. Oh! And Pantomime.

Today the Opera House is still as innovative. On the comedy side, a favourite, often treading the Buxton boards was the late comedian Ken Dodd with his Happiness Show.

The tickets to his show were the only ones printed which said 7.30pm till late! Pauline Case had the pleasure of seeing him I quote. "Brilliant", he was a bugger, we didn't leave till 12.30 am.

The Roaring Twenties and Turbulent Thirties

After the 1st World War John Mottershead travelled to London where he became an Opera exhibitioner at the Ernest Palmer Royal College of Music. He did concert oratorio work, made several classical records and had many classical roles in various productions. In 1928, John married Elsie French while they were playing together in 'The Rose and the Ring' at the Apollo theatre, London.

They travelled to America in 1931, touring in 'The Beggar's Opera', John playing Macheath and Elsie, Mrs Peachum. It was at this time that John shortened his name to Mott.

On the 18th October 1932 John and Elsie made their first appearance as the "Aspidistras", singing serious Victorian songs with sympathetic satire. The venue was a navy league matinee at Westminster Theatre, London. HRH, Princess Louise, Duchess of Argyle was in attendance. The Aspidistras were now becoming well known in London's theatre land, playing at many top venues such as The Westminster, Shaftesbury, Ambassador, Cambridge and Wyndham theatres.

In the 1930s, the early days of black and white television, Aspidistra photographs were often seen in the BBC Radio Times, many newspapers and magazines. There was only one TV channel showing with programmes for two hours daily, 2pm to 3pm and 9pm to 10pm. John and Elsie often appeared twice in one day. When ITV started, John appeared in commercials, including one for baked beans.

During the war the Aspidistras did their bit, regulars at The Players Theatre which started in 1936. John and Elsie joined in 1939 soon becoming its backbone. They helped to keep it open, along with the Windmill, throughout the world war. The only two theatres to manage this during the bombing raids.

In December 1940 they were in three daily shows, Wyndham's in the afternoons; Players Theatre, Ablemarle Street in the evening; later on to Berkeley Street where the Mayfair Hotel, was helping to keep spirits high in wartime London. On opening night the Aspidistras made history by persuading 290 diners to dance the polka with them.

Sir Oswald Stoll booked them at the Colosseum in "Diversion" having seen the Aspidistras in the first edition of this production a year earlier at the Wyndham theatre. As well as the Aspidistras performing, John also did a one man show entitled "Father and Son". It was one of only three shows in London during 1941.

John and Elsie also made documentaries for the Ministry of Food "Time to Remember" and "Christmas under Fire".

Many top hotels such as the Savoy, Berkeley, Dorchester, and the Ritz were featuring them in cabaret, making them household names of the Mayfair set.

In 1944 they toured Italy and Africa with E.N.S.A entertaining the troops. During this time they witnessed the last big eruption of Vesuvius on the 19th March 1944, with Joyce Grenfell, after having supper with her.

The Aspidistras played their last engagement in Brussels, with the Temperance Seven in February 1966, (ending 34 years of performances) once again in front of Royalty, The King of Belgium.

As for John's siblings, George, Jessie and Lydia. George became secretary of the North Staffordshire Royal Infirmary and lived in Stoke on Trent. Jessie and Lydia were also musical and were the leading

ladies in the B.A.D.O.S productions at the Opera House each year, which was so important during the 1920s and 30s. They sang duets and solos at concerts in the Pavilion Gardens and local hotels, being part of the Higher Buxton Quartet with whom they won numerous prizes at musical festivals in Buxton, Matlock, Stoke and Blackpool.

Jessie and Lydia also won prizes for their duets and solos. For many years I went to sleep at night to the sound of them rehearsing... mostly Gilbert and Sullivan songs.

Lydia was in the "Women's Royal Voluntary Service"during WWII. She organised concerts every Sunday evening for the Troops at the Buxton Town Hall canteen. My sister Mary sang "A Child's Prayer" solo and local musical families would also perform at these concerts.

When my mother Jessie married Arthur Jackson on the 13th April 1924 the headline in the Buxton Advertiser was "Abigail Weds". She had taken the lead as Abigail at the Opera House, in "The Rebel Maid" earlier that year.

Flying Forties and Nifty Fifties

Jimmy Munroe and the QCs on stage at the Pavilion Gardens.

Were a local orchestral band formed in the 1940s/50s. Jimmy is at the fore with his Clarinet. On drums is Joe Mortin. According to George Wilshaw, Jimmy would frequent the British Legion in the 1970s/ 80s. His conversations were always interesting and he was a gentleman.

Dave Attwood

Here are some of the Dance bands in Buxton from the late 50s to the 70s. The number of Pop groups was certainly a lot more. The GQs, named after George Henrique, who financed the band, were a Big

Band resident at the Spa Hotel.

1. High Peak Swing Band (still going).
2. Black Cats.
3. Ray Pickering Band.
4. Dave Turner Five, later called, Dave Turner Sound.
5. Cliff Lack Band - resident band at the Anglers Rest, Bamford.
6. John Granger and the Peaklanders.
7. Colin Sellers Trio.
8. John Smith - Take Two.
9. Alf White Band.
10. Pat Moone and Blue Axis.
11. Spa Trio.
12. The Graham Robinson Band.

There were resident musicians at all the local clubs as well. The Liberal Club, Spa Bar, Working Men's, (aka the Working Mens Club), Bus Club, Great Rocks Club, Sterndale Moor Club, Whaley Bridge Bowling Club, Harpur Hill Club, Chapel Memorial Club and Tideswell Club.

And less than three and a half miles away, Peak Dale village had its share of professional dance band musicians: Nigel Carter (Trumpet) with the BBC big band. Roy Carter (Tenor Sax) with the Ken Mackintosh Band and Ken Turner (Trumpet) Blackpool Tower band.

In the late 1970s, Buxton's Geoff White Quintet (Geoff on violin, Barry Bryant bass, Derrick Buxton rhythm guitar, Billy Street lead guitar and Dave Attwood drums) played most Sundays at the Queens Arms pub in Taddington near Buxton. Unbeknownst to the band, one of the customers there had entered them for an audition in Manchester for Opportunity Knocks.

In the first instance, no way were any of the band going to do that BUT over a few pints it was decided that as a fun day out they would go. Much to their surprise Hughie Green invited them to play on Opportunity Knocks in London on Thames TV. They came 1st on the Clapometer and second in the public vote. They were offered professional work and made a couple of recordings but nothing really came of it. There was the occasional murmur about a Buxton band being on television but that was about it.

One thing they did find out from that trip was that Hughie Green was no stranger to Buxton. He was a fighter pilot with the Canadian Air Force and spent several months at the Empire Hotel in Buxton to recuperate after being shot down over England in the Second World War. The Empire Hotel had been requisitioned by the armed forces for such purposes.

Dave has been associated with and played with many bands in the Manchester area. He was leader of the High Peak Swing Band for many years playing either Drums or Saxophone. The High Peak Swing Band, with whom he has played for 25 years, still play today.

Taken from Dave's set list

THE SAUNTER 32 bar
Foxtrot Red Rose Saunter,
Sandringham Saunter.

THE WALTZ 32 bar Modern Waltz
Apple Blossom Waltz,
Denverdale Waltz.

OLDE TIME WALTZ
Pride of Erin Waltz,
Viennese Swing.

QUICK STEPS – 32 bar quickstep
Saffron Swing,

Manhattan Blues.

CHA CHA-32 bars
Jackpot (cha cha)
Sally-Ann cha cha.

FOX TROTS- 32 bar
Shanty blues (bright)
Jasmine foxtrot.

RUMBA
Rumba Valentino
Rumba No. 1.

OTHERS
Hoop-a-la
Mambo Magic (slow Mambo rhythm).

Saturday Morning Pictures

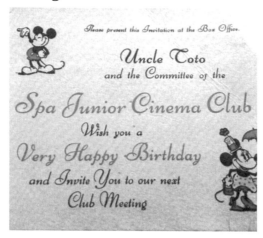

Kathleen Eperson was born in Buxton. As a young girl growing up in the 1950s, she was mad about the children's Saturday morning pictures held at the Spa Cinema. There was one drawback, the entrance fee. The years after the Second World War money was tight for most people so she wasn't always able to go.

Then she had an idea. Being fairly observant, she had noticed that the St. Ann's Well drinking cup was not the most desirable receptacle for visitors to drink from. The cup was heavy and cumbersome, made of pewter and chained to the stone of the Well.

Her idea resulted in getting herself a glass tumbler, settling down at the Well and charging a halfpenny to passers-by and tourists for the use of the glass. Much more preferable to the heavy chained cup.

Her cost to the cinema was covered. Then disaster... she was spotted by Aunt Flo! When Kathleen arrived home, she got a good telling off and told never to do that sort of thing again.

Mum, having realised Kathleen's plight, presented her with a paid subscription to join the children's film club. She was over the moon. The Club was called Uncle Toto's.

On your birthday the other children members would sing "Happy Birthday" to you. Also Uncle Toto would give you a ice lolly, it was always banana flavour and I hated it. As you were at the front you had to eat it!

Saturday Morning Pictures. Spa Cinema 1958. Henry Buxton, the cinema Managing Director presenting a prize. Janet and her twin sisters, Ann and Carol Hobson are pictured.

On Saturday morning's her dad would give her 2 shilling and 6 pence. Passing Thorpe's sweet shop she would pop in to get sweets to eat in the cinema. Disaster struck one day when she dropped the money down a grid. Luckily a passer by lifted the lid and retrieved it. The delay meant, the queue to get in would be winding its way up Holker Road.

Her next great passion was roller skating. This was held in the Octagon, Pavilion Gardens. You were able to hire roller skates but these were very basic and not very fast. Many had their own which had often been bought as birthday or Christmas presents. Kathleen would go as often as she could.

Records would be played as the skaters chased, made long chains, dodged round the pillars, performing their skills, at the same time avoiding the beginners who were having a job to stay on their feet.

It was a meeting place for all the town's children, teens and adults.

Roller Energy. Buxton Community School. 2020.

The Swinging Sixties

And swinging it certainly was! The Pavilion Ballroom was the "In Place", attracting fans from far and wide and especially us Buxtonians.

In the early 1960s Beat music, British beat, and the Merseybeat was formed. Luckily for us, the Entertainment management must have been going through a lucrative period judging by the amount of entertainment Buxton had in the Pavilion Gardens for the next three years.

1961: One of the bands The Pavilion Gardens played host to was Eric Delaney and his Band. Mr Acker Bilk and his Band appeared in this year. (Stranger on the Shore).

1962: There was a Saturday club called 'Twistacutor.' (not for squares).

Taken from a paragraph in the Buxton Advertiser:

On Saturday April the 26th 1962 the Beatles will appear at the Pavilion Gardens.

The Beatles crashed into the disc charts with their first release. At the moment they are hits where ever they go. Their latest release is, A side Please Please Me. B side Ask Me Why.

At this time they were not very well known so the audience was sparse but the Pavilion Gardens rebooked them for 1963. By that time they were a internationally famed pop group. Luckily they honoured their contract.

The Pavilion capacity was 100 people but, 1,200 attended.

Snippet

Though the venue was full, a queue of people stretched from the Kings Head, all the way down Hall Bank to the Pavilion Gardens entrance.

1963: Two of the bands to play that year were The Beatles and Gerry and the Pacemakers, both originating from Liverpool.

*Local man, Barry Blood was a
member of 'The Trixons'.*

Harry Hopper Band. L to R Barry Blood, Neil Tatum, Pauline Saldate, Gary Mitchell and Colin Bramwell.

In the late Sixties Colin Bramwell and his friend Jonn Goodwin had a mobile disco called Plastic Dream. One of their venues, being the Ashwood, now a Wetherspoons called The Wye Bridge.

In 1973 Barry was with the popular Harry Hopper Band. They toured Germany, May to July 1973.

1964: The Searchers and the Foremost... two more Merseybeat groups. Billy J Kramer and the Dakotas were remembered by Kathleen Eperson. She was at the front, next to the stage with her friend Beryl. During the performance, Billy leant over to the fans and in a flash, Beryl cut his tie off for a 'souvenir'.

1965: Bands such as: The Who, The Pretty Things, The Animals, The Kinks and the Walker Brothers.

Linda Slater recalls: I wanted to go and see the Kinks and my Mum said I couldn't go to the concert. On the day, I remember telling her I was going for a walk with the dog. I met up with two of my friends, Vicky Rains and Yvonne Eyre (maiden names). We sneaked in the Pavilion grounds by way of a loose railing. The gardens then, was completely enclosed by iron railings. Prior to the show we knocked on the dressing room door. Ray Davis (lead singer and Rhythm guitar) let us in. The dressing room was small and cramped.

After a few minutes a chap came in saying the lads had to get ready as it was nearly time to go on stage. It was a quick stage left from us.

The Walker Brothers from America played at the Pavilion Gardens on 2nd October 1965. I can say "I was there", aged fourteen years and five months old. Not very tall and green behind the ears. There I was, squashed up toward the front, with neck craned. Looking toward the stage I see long skinny legs, tight jeans and a drum kit at the back. My ears are buzzing with their sound and Scott Walker singing leading vocals. Another thing I recall is the eight pillars in the hall. Standing on tiptoe amidst the crowd, peering and crushed round.

The headline in the local paper following the Pretty Things concert read. "It Was The Beatles All Over Again" and "Pretty Things Start A Riot". Apparently when the band started to perform, screaming girls invaded the stage trying to get close to their idols, causing mayhem. The St. John Ambulance Brigade treated 24 girls for shock.

Later, Phil May's stage contortions brought more screams and girls surging forward, keeping stage staff busy, rushing them off through side doors.

Not only was there activity at the concert but the Police had been tipped off about a vengeance gang fight in retaliation to Buxton youths two weeks previously. New Mills and Chapel-en-le-Frith youths had got together and were expected in Buxton that night. Luckily it was a false alarm.

1966: The Beat Sound was waning and a host of different sounds were beginning to emerge. Manfred Mann, Small Faces (one of my faves) and the Yardbirds would make appearances.

1969: On the 26th September an all-night Blues Festival was held in the Pavilion Gardens. Fleetwood Mac were on the bill and it is said they played one of their biggest hits, "Albatross" for the first time.

70s Disco Era *(many a "muso" would question that)*

Darren Sherwin

My dad was a car sprayer working for Kennings. The spray shop was alongside The Railway Hotel and beneath the railway bridge. When I was ten years old he came home with tickets which his friend Steve Robinson had given him. The two were for the Rock Festival at Booth Farm over at Brandside, Buxton.

It was 1973 and I was 10 years old, imagine how I felt. The stage had been erected on a kind of larger bunker which probably had been used by the RAF, quarrying or the mines research.

Being just 10, I felt so small amongst such a huge crowd which included all types of young people, including "Hell's Angels" who I remembered caused havoc by mounting the stage, causing Chuck Berry to walk off not to return.

The Sensational Alex Harvey Band opened up with "Crazy Horses" an Osmonds number of all things, but it sure got the festival going. The Edgar Broughton Band spoke these words before starting their set, "I want you to see me, I want you to feel me" and as a ten year old that made an impression that I still feel today with my love of live music, music and concerts.

The following year I was in luck again. Another surprise, and another two tickets for me and my dad. Now I am a year older, much more aware and ready for the experience. I still have the treasured original programme which I bought. I lived up Harpur Hill at the time, residents were lining the road hoping to catch a glimpse of Rod Stewart or any other "rock star" as they made their way along the back roads to Booth

Farm. The weather turned atrocious, worse than the previous year. I remember Afghan coats, everybody wrapped up, mud and fear of electrocution on the stage, due to the wind and rain.

After the concert was abandoned, thousands made their way home. Scores walked into Buxton, freezing and wrapped up in wet clothes. Churches, School Rooms, homes and numerous other places of refuge opened their doors to give them warmth, hot food and drink. Even the bands had their problems. "Nazareth" pulled up at the Manchester Arms only to be refused entry by the landlord, because of their muddy attire and boots. When told who they were, the landlord replied "I don't give a bugger who thee are!"

Overend Watts, Mott the Hoople.

My favourite band of 74 was Mott the Hoople. I later contacted them and built up a correspondence with guitarist Overend Watts.

Ironically this festival was Mott the Hoople's last gig on main-land Britain. Although they reunite in 2008 and played 6 gigs at Hammersmith, London. Prior to this they did a warm up gig in Monmouth. I was there and met the band. We chatted and reminisced about Buxton 1974. "They remembered it well"!

This is me taken with Ariel Bender (Mott the Hoople) in Manchester 2019. His real name Luther Grovenor. Like at our meeting before, we reminisced about when they headlined the Festival in 1974. The rain and the mud... but what a night they had. It was to be their last show in the UK.

This postcard below is from the headmaster of Burbage School thanking me and Dave Fawkes playing at my daughter Phoebe's school assembly. We played five Elvis songs in front of 360 children. The kids were all singing, clapping and making a heck of a noise. What a great day, we even had to scratch together an encore. We only practised five numbers up at Dave's house. We really enjoyed ourselves. Sadly, this was to be Dave's last gig.

Snippet courtesy of Don Mycock

BRANDSIDE... 4 miles out of Buxton has been home to the Mycock family, working and schooling there since the 1900s.

BOOTH FARM... home to George Mycock who married Joan Smith, they had five children, Ronald, Gilda, Carol, Shirley and Cathy.

TURNCLIFFE FARM... Beryl (daughter of above Ronald Mycock) who married Arthur Smith and their three children Gillian, Philip and Susan.

GREEN SIDES FARM... Thomas and Rose Mycock with their three children Dennis, George and Beryl.

THIRKLOW FARM... Dennis Mycock who married Ann Grindey from Longnor, they had six children Don, Linda, Sandra, David, Ken and Roy.

Dave "Elvis" Fawkes

Ian Fawkes

Any man of a certain age, in their 40s, 50s, 60s and beyond will probably remember the barbers on Market Street in Buxton and will have probably frequented it at some time in their lives. It was called The Waldorf Saloon and was run by Dave Fawkes but of course to a great many more people he was known as Dave "Elvis" Fawkes. Of course Dave was a massive (exaggeration there) Elvis fan and the barbers shop could best be described as a shrine to Elvis. Oh, and by the way Dave is my Uncle.

When my sister and myself were infants we would often go and stay on a Saturday night at our Grandma and Grandad's at Sterndale Moor whilst our Mum and Dad went out to Sterndale Moor Club. Uncle Dave would often by getting ready when we arrived to go out on a "gig". This was the swinging sixties and Dave would be dressed accordingly in suit and tie. He would get ready, grab his guitar, my Grandad would say even at the age I was. At 7, 8 or 9, I was getting the bug for music. Uncle Dave would kindly let me thumb through and play his vast record collection, because I was hooked on The Yardbirds, fairly unusual for one so young. The seeds of a future in music for me were sown.

Anyway eventually I was allowed across the road to the club to see a Dave "Elvis" gig and I was not disappointed. He did the full Elvis show, wore the gear, played the songs and pulled a crowd. People would travel to see him and go crazy at the gigs. He could sing like Elvis and always made sure the music was right. He was a master of the guitar, in fact he was a "chord" man and to watch him go up and down the fretboard to find the correct chord was a treat to behold. He played mainly locally but did sometimes travel. He was asked by the Elvis Presley Fan Club to do the Elvis Convention and was so well received he was asked back time and time again. He did commit his tribute to vinyl under the band name "Compendium" which is well worth seeking out.

Of course sometimes going into the Waldorf saloon could be an experience in itself and if the shop was empty you'd often find Dave sat playing a tune on his guitar. A friend told me one Christmas Eve they'd been out at lunch time and decided to call in on the way home and see if Dave would play them "Blue Christmas". He had a young lad in the chair whose hair he'd half cut but couldn't resist playing the song, so with the lad looking terrified Dave played the song with added vocals from my friend and his mates. That was Dave.

Of course he was a massive influence on me and has always offered encouragement to me and the bands that I have played in. Yes, Uncle Dave does go down as a local music legend, his like will probably be never seen again. Just like The Waldorf Saloon ask anyone of a certain age and they will know of Dave "Elvis" Fawkes.

Snippet

Ian Fawkes followed in his uncle Dave's musical footsteps. He is lead singer and harmonica player for the local band Route 66. He has played at all the local venues and pubs many times. They also travel across the country with bookings and festivals.

Alas due to the covid virus, like everything else gigging is mothballed. Over the years they have done more than 1200 gigs since forming in 1989.

Snippet

I recall a good night of mine, in the 1990s at the Bus Club, Scarsdale Place. Route 66 were playing, they were on top form and the place was rocking. When we came to leave my friends and I had to take it steady down the lethal stairs.

Les Hallam

One of the first mobile discos was 'Blue Grass' disco formed by Les Hallam and Pete Lucas in 1969. They continued until September 1970. A spin off from this was a regular Wednesday night disco at Harpur Hill Club for under 18s which ran from April to September 1970. In the very early 70s Kevin Allsop did discos in a youth club and very soon was asked to do various parties, so turned mobile. He finished in 1980 but for many years, he often helped out other discos when they were busy at Christmas.

In 1973 two popular discos came on the Buxton scene. Spread Eagle Disco was formed by Phil Pitts and Robert Wagstaffe. They were big on the Northern Soul circuit. Nigel Parker joined them in 1976 and eventually took over until 1985. Also that year JAM Disco was formed an abbreviation of John Allen Music. John left Buxton in October 1979 but returned to do one last Xmas party at the St. Anne's Hotel in December!

In 1974 Les Hallam and Wes Portas formed 'Osmosis' Disco. Probably the most versatile disco of the time playing everything from Heavy Rock nights to a complete evening of Ballroom dancing but mainly chart music or a complete mix. They became the most booked Buxton disco of the 70's. They finished in 1981.

Inspired by Osmosis, John Read (his words!) and Dave Gladwin formed '2001' Disco in 1975. They were together until 1979 when John teamed up with Steve Kay to form 'Nebulous One' Disco. John left Buxton in 1984 and Steve continued their success until 1988.

Late 70s and early 80s saw three other local discos appear on the Buxton scene. 'Cloud Sound' Disco run by Nigel Harby and Paul Timmins, 'Carmina Burana' Disco run by Dave Neville (who eventually ran many regular weekly discos in Buxton involving himself and guest DJs) and Robert Evans 'High Voltage Disco. High Voltage became a true Roadshow able to cope with large venues with a massive sound and lightshow. Robert called it a day in 1995.

In 1982 Les Hallam returned with 'Trilogy' Disco. Establishing quickly on the same format of his previous disco 'Osmosis'. Finishing in 1987 his son Dan Hallam soon took over as 'Son of Trilogy'. Dan performed for 10 years between 1990 and 2000. Dan soon established himself as a student DJ.

EAT   SLEEP   RAVE   REPEAT

Mark Merrick

In the early 90s the music scene started to change in Buxton with Paul Smith and Eddie Chapman introducing us to the sounds from Chicago and Holland with House and Techno music upstairs at The Clubhouse.

This led to various open air raves in various Derbyshire beauty spots being organised by Black Moon Sound System + MAD, such as The Goyt Valley, Monsal Trails Tunnels and the Temple of Troms.

It also led Mark Merrick (Mez) to start up a house music night with Dean Hammond & various other Guests every month in the back room of The Railway Hotel - The night was called MAD.

The Temple of Troms was a big highlight for Buxton's partygoers and is still talked about to this day. The large lay by at Lovers Leap was three deep in raver's cars - whilst many a hardy Buxtonian walked the roads there and back - for some the memory of the walk is just as big a highlight as the rave itself!

With the popularity of the regular MAD nights. MAD also ran special one off events throughout the year.

One particular event - Millennium Eve very nearly wasn't meant to be but the night was saved by a local business man Robert Critchlow.

Initially the party had been arranged to take place in a local disused church but on the morning of the party the police got wind of it and made a visit to Mark Merrick and made it very clear to him that there was going to be NO party. This was a nightmare. Over 200 tickets had gone out and with hours to spare - but now no venue!

Out of the blue, Mark got a call from an unknown number asking to meet outside Bargain Booze. Mark met with Robert Critchlow who before this time was unknown to him. Robert had got wind of the cancelled party and in his words said 'People of Buxton are not going to have their Millennium Eve ruined by Bigoted Police'. Robert offered Mark the use of an empty warehouse so the party could go ahead.

The first floor warehouse which was located just off the high street was no Church but it certainly did the job. Two hundred plus ravers squeezed into a small warehouse (total sweat pit) with one toilet and floorboards that shook with the sheer weight.

The party was a success and the best way to see in the Millennium. Mark always says that after this Robert Critchlow became his hero.

The Noughties

In 2005 with the new licensing hours, entertainment took a new curve. More late night venues for bands and DJs. Alongside this was Club Acoustic held at the Clubhouse, and open Mic nights.

Terry Dann

I came to Buxton as a contractor working on the new cement plant at BLI, 2003. I loved this town, reminded of a mini Liverpool with some of the surrounding architecture. I ended moving here in 2005 I moved into a flat above the Eagle pub and I used to hear music being played from my flat above. Intrigued. I went down into the pub and it was.

The late great Chris Rockliffe acoustic sessions. I became friends with the manager Craig France and I asked him how often these music nights took place and he said every fortnight. So I asked him what was on in between. He said nothing. So I said, would he be interested if I supplied a full PA. Full drum kit, amps and guitars for local people to come in and on the condition that the younger talented youths could come and play as long as they were with their parents. He said give it a go, so I did. Within a month the Eagle became what was known locally as Rock Night at the Eagle.

It was heaving with pure musical talent and mostly teenagers, from drummers, guitarists, singers, bassists and for the majority of them it was their first chance they ever got to play real instruments live on stage in front of an audience. Each week just got better and busier. These musicians were now bonding as friends and as band members forming bands and learning off each other. There are a few bands that are still together now that formed through the rock nights and friendships were created from it also.

Anyhow through that and over the years I myself got to meet a lot of local talented musicians and with Facebook being a great platform to advertise. I thought it would be a good idea to start "The Buxton Musicians Page". As you can see in the. About section. It's about coming together and sharing your musical skills and talents with the wider community and musically minded people. The group is a great one. Never had anyone ever making nasty comments. It's just grown and grown. With almost 750 followers on the page from all musical walks of life. The Buxton Musicians page is a great local hub to share your up and coming gigs. Videos and photos past and present and also advertising the selling instruments. I've been here in Buxton now for 17 years and I can honestly say I love this town and its people. But most of all I love how it has so many talented people and characters.

Local band Fuzzy Felt World playing in the Pavilion Gardens at distance June 2020.

I HAD HEARD THAT LAURENCE LLEWELYN BOWEN WAS IN TOWN

White Hall: Activities.

THE GREAT OUTDOORS

Buxton's prime position in the Derbyshire landscape has for centuries attracted people drawn to the great outdoors. The sights and amenities are boundless. Just out of Buxton we have White Hall which opened in 1951 as Britain's first local education authority outdoor centre. Today it is still active, catering for youth and schools.

1951 also was the year the first National Park was opened, and yes, it was the Peak District. 2121 will see White Hall celebrating its seventy years of service.

Dave Alsop was born in Buxton 1936, spending his childhood in Heath Grove, and attending Hardwick Square and Kents Bank schools.

When he was 18, Dave joined up for National Service. He was stationed with the Royal Electrical and Mechanical Engineer Engineers. On finishing his duties he came back to Buxton and worked as an Electrician.

Dave had always been keen on local history, community and outdoor pursuits around the area. In 1961 he was prompted to found the Derbyshire Cave Rescue Organization. This followed the tragic death of Neil Moss, in Peak Cavern, Castleton. Dave was one of the last people to reach Neil while he was still alive. Over the years he was personally involved in more than 100 rescues and saving countless lives.

Dave Alsop.

Dave set a new world record in 1962 after leading the first successful British expedition to Gouffre Berger cave in the French Alps. Amongst the team were three men from Buxton. These were Mick Mullen, Mike Poulten and Tony Huntingdon from the Eldon Pot Hole Club.

In 1976 Dave was contracted to do some wiring work at Pooles Cavern. It was whilst working there that he saw the potential to reopen the old tourist attraction, which he and others managed to do.

Sure enough he was given the job of Warden in 1976, until he retired in 1977. Dave was married to local girl Brenda Heathcote, a local girl who was one of four children. Dave and Brenda had two children, Carol and Ian.

Sam Townsend in Bagshawe Cavern. Photo by Rob Eavis, 2018.

Eldon pothole Club, Albania, 2010.

Nostalgia Isn't What It Used To Be

Wacker (Brian Woodall)

Formed in the late 1950s by some small local caving enthusiasts, the Eldon Pothole Club is one of the foremost Caving Clubs in Derbyshire.

We attracted potholers from all over the country and especially several University cavers. Of course this led to a bit of an accommodation problem. So early on we obtained an upper floor premises at the back of Spring Gardens which was accessed by a ladder. When a lady visitor once enquired where the toilet was, she was directed to the ladder.

The hostel was handily situated next to a late-night drinking establishment called the Barbecue. This place developed a reputation for serving a lethal cocktail containing several alcohols, mixes and more alcohols until it tasted just like a strawberry milkshake - lethal!

As well as having some wonderful cave systems and mines to explore at home, and because we were bang central in the country we could easily travel up to the magnificent potholes in the Yorkshire Dales. These included the wonderful waterfalls in Gaping Gill. Then at Easter time we could easily get down the long long cave passageways of Aggy O.F.D. and Dany-Ogof. Camping and potholing can be a bit bracing, especially when you have to pull on a damp wet-suit on a frosty morning in South Wales.

Spring Bank Holidays were often spent camping on the old Lead Works on the Mineries near Priddy in Somerset. (but watch out for adders!). From here we could access St Cutherbert's Swallet or systems such as Swiddons, Eastwater or Stoke Lane Slocket. One of the main attractions was the Queen Victoria on Priddy Fair Day. Here, new members to Mendip Caving Club were initiated into the scene by drinking their age in pints through the day. Nineteen was considered to be the optimum age for this venture.

Later in the 1960s the Eldon Club took over running a hut in the heart of the slate mining country in North Wales. The hut was converted from the offices of a huge slate mine. We could walk just 200 yards directly into a system of levels and massive galleries which took you right through the mountain to daylight on the other side. There were masses of old material lying about, and coming down at some height from one of the terraces was a thick steel hawser rope. With the aid of a parachute rope and steel shackles, the Eldon converted this into a very early form of zip-wire. It was most impressive after dark when showers of steel sparks came of the shackle as we hurtled down the hawser.

The club made up the main part of Team C (central team) of the Derbyshire Cave Rescue Organization, and were involved in a huge amount of rescues over the years. These included the failed attempt to extricate Neil Moss from a crevice in Peak Cavern. On a lighter note, we were involved in the epic (and successful) 24hr rescue of Donna Carr from the bottom of Giants Hole in 1965.

In 1964 the club made up a large part of a group led by Dave Allsop to become the first National team to bottom the world's deepest cave, the Gouffre Berger in France.

It wasn't all hard work though. In the mid-60s there were many Rock n Roll bands around and we gathered quite a reputation. "Perhaps we weren't quite the hardest caving club around - but we did have the best "stomps". We would have the upstairs room in the White Lion hosted by Jack and Martha. There were quite a lot of 21st Birthdays coming up about then and it was the Birthday Boy's treat to lay on a barrel of beer. All the thanks he got was to be debagged during a stomp. However the floor was covered in a soft lino, and what with all the beer being spilled/ thrown, the floor became a pink soup. It paid not to come in anything posh to an Eldon Stomp. By the end of the night, when the band had finished off with "Satisfaction", Jack the landlord would reel onto the floor with "Time to go home ladies and gentlemen... I don't make the laws. Mr Wilson makes the laws" (that last bit should be read with a slurring accent).

Our group became quite famous for parties, either organising them, being invited to them or even sometimes gate crashing them. But it was always peacefully and with good humour. One Saturday night, sat drinking in the Eldon room at the Eagle Hotel, some youth ran in and cried "I'm having a party at my house". They all sat around like dummies. "Could you all please come and liven it up a bit?" Well... anything to oblige! For a while afterwards we called ourselves "Rent a Party"!

We also put on a bit of a show in 1970 when we abseiled from the Spring Gardens viaduct and down onto the carnival below. But time waits for no-one, the hostel and the Barbecue were swept away in the building of the new Shopping Arcade. Cavers became more serious, stomps started to thin out and we were no longer singing rude songs in sympathetic hostelries around the country. Time to vegetate.

Snippet

As a girl of 16 or 17, I found myself and my friend Linda Slater passing the White Lion. We entered, we danced, got soaked and my white trousers turned red. On my arrival home, Mum and Dad were waiting up. You can guess the rest.

Caving Supplies. The Story.

Phil Brown

Caving Supplies was started in 1972, and moved to Buxton in 1976. Buxton was chosen as an ideal location where Phil & Chandra could raise their two daughters, and expand their business further. An old grocery corner shop was purchased, with plenty of room for storage, and with a two storey dwelling above.

In June 1976 on a cold grey day, a large lorry packed to the roof with household contents and business stock made it's way to Buxton, driven by Mick Knott, a friendly caving customer and lorry driver. Phil & Chandra with their two children, a one year old and a three year old, following close behind.

Cavers from the TSG caving club in Castleton helped unload the lorry and ferry everything into the building. Phil was most grateful for the help, because he was exhausted after two days filling the lorry and driving up to Derbyshire.

Initially business was very quiet, in 1976 there was no internet, no mobile phone and the caving magazine Descent wasn't published for months. A Mail Order catalogue was produced and sent to existing customers, which got the business growing nicely.

Then along came the Callaghan "crisis what crisis" government and the economy slowed right down, which meant the shop was hardly selling anything. Phil (ex mobile mechanic) said he was at the point where he was going to cruise the main roads and motorways looking for breakdowns to try and earn some money to survive. Just at the point the business would have had to close, it started picking up. Sales started rising and once again the business was viable. Now growing at an amazing rate, 30-40% year on year, with the shop open seven days a week.

It was like riding a roller coaster where you never got to the top of the first climb, it just went up and up. There were no holidays for eight years until eventually the first employee was taken on. Another employee was taken on to pack parcels for Mail Order and serve in the shop. A sewing machinist was taken on to sew Caving Belts, Harnesses, Helmet Head Cradles and Chin Straps, Tackle Bags, Webbing Slings, then another sewing machinist to cope with the growing range of products.

The business grew through the 1970s and into the 1980s and various special opportunities presented themselves which helped provide funding for further expansion at a key time. One notable opportunity occurred as follows.

Cavers are an ingenious bunch, and good at finding economical ways to buy their equipment. Someone had noticed that government surplus Ex. RAF fighter aircraft batteries could be fitted into old lead-acid mining lamp battery cases. This worked well because externally the lamp looked and worked the same, internally the battery was now a high capacity alkaline battery which reliably gave 20 hours of light.

Phil managed to purchase large numbers of these batteries from ex military auctions and spent several hours a day for over a year cleaning and preparing the batteries for sale in the shop. The profit generated from the sale of these batteries helped fund the purchase of other stock which in turn helped the business to grow further.

During 1981 Caving Supplies started looking at computer systems to help control the fast growing stock inventory. This was well before personal computers started to become popular during the 1990's. The first Caving Supplies computer had two x 1 megabyte disc drives, each 1mb drive was about twice the physical size of a modern computer. The new computer enabled a high turnover of customer orders and helped control the rapidly growing business.

In 1983, a local building came up for sale that Caving Supplies could use as a warehouse to store an expanding range of products, and house a range of low priced job lots that came up from time to time. The building provided 4,500 square feet on two floors, and included several garages. The building was purchased and readied for Caving Supplies use, just in time for a very large delivery of boots.

The British Standard for safety boots had changed, and a manufacturers stock no longer complied with the new standard. 3,000 pairs of boots were available cheap, but you had to buy them all. Caving Supplies conveniently had plenty of warehouse space to store them, over 5 tons of boots in total. It took six months to make back the cost price of the boots. Cavers got a good product for a knock down price, and Caving Supplies made a good profit, helping fund more new products.

During 1985, Phil & Chandra enjoyed an occasional meal with local friends. One day Paul phoned Caving Supplies and said his company had some Rocket Tubes for sale, there were a few hundred, did they want to buy any? Paul's company had bought the tubes to hold specialized cement samples for testing, but then decided to use something else.

The Rocket Tubes were robust plastic with a screw lid, designed to contain a specific type of military ammunition. The shop already sold Rocket Tubes, and cavers were buying them on a regular basis to carry items of photographic equipment etc. The price would be 50p each for 250 pieces.

Paul said he could deliver them with their works van. The first vanload was for around 500 pieces, then another vanload, about six vanloads in all. Paul didn't want payment for the extra tubes, just as long as Caving Supplies could take them all because he needed the space. Nice, it took about three years to sell all the tubes.

In 1986 the Premier Lamp Company went bust. They used to make acetylene lamps powered by Calcium Carbide which makes Acetylene gas when mixed with water, and provided an intense white light popular with cavers. Caving Supplies was a regular customer for these lights and sold many hundreds to cavers over the years.

Phil heard the company had gone bust and phoned the Liquidator to enquire if any of the tools were for sale. The liquidator was happy to sell the tooling and spare parts, approx 10 tons weight mainly in the tooling. £3,000 was agreed and a lorry organized to collect the tooling and deliver to Buxton.

A few days later the phone rang, and the Liquidator asked if 50 x Premier King lamps were of interest, all boxed up brand new ready for sale. Phil offered £50 for the lot, which the liquidator accepted. Liquidators don't seem interested in how much money they make, as long as they manage to get rid of everything. In the event the lamps were sold for £50 each, making around £2,500 in just six months.

As manufacturing started Caving Supplies received phone calls from companies in Nigeria and Ghana to buy acetylene lamps. Wonderful, customers buying 500 – 1000 pieces per order were just what was needed. The lamps were used for hunting animals who are apparently attracted by the light. A second assembly worker was taken on and over the years tens of thousands of lamps were made. Eventually the Nigerian inflation rate became so great they couldn't afford to buy the product.

Other opportunities came and went, and various events caused a decline in caver numbers. There were fewer new cavers buying complete sets of caving gear, and new faces were definitely the bread and butter that kept the shop busy.

Student Unions wanted Insurance, to get insurance they needed cave leaders, to be a cave leader took four years, by which time the cave leader had left university. As the decline increased there were fewer new faces to keep the business going.

An activity centre owner was convicted of gross negligence when four teenagers drowned on a kayak trip across Lyme Bay. This incident accelerated governmental discussions to end self-regulation of outdoor education centres, leading to a significant decline in young people being taken on outdoor activities including caving, which caused a massive reduction in caver numbers over the years.

In 2001 the sheep Foot & Mouth disease outbreak stopped people going into the countryside, and some cavers never returned to the sport.

Between 1991-2011 Radon was found to be present in relatively high levels in popular caves. County Council Outdoor Centres instructors were getting high radiation doses in just a few trips, so caving was gradually closed down, resulting in fewer "taster" caving trips which had introduced people to caving.

Amongst all the bad news there was very little good news leading to any increase in sales of Caving equipment, so Phil had to think hard how he might expand the business into new areas. At this stage Chandra (Phil's wife) was running the admin side of the business, packing parcels, and serving in the shop, while Phil looked after the sewing and manufacturing side together with business development.

In 2001 Phil set up a division within the company called Rope Access Supplies. Commercial customers were window cleaners of tall buildings, installers of glass cladding on buildings like the Shard in London, Installation, Servicing and De-commissioning of wind turbines, the Fire Service and a whole range of specialist Steeple Jack companies. Other companies were using the services of Rope Access Technicians, who could do jobs traditionally done by people working out of cradles or from cranes, but access on rope was quicker and more economical.

The Caving business continued at a lower level than in earlier years, with the business overheads supported by the expanding Rope Access business, which kept the company extremely busy until 2020 when Covid-19 arrived.

The lockdown initiated by the government to minimise the spread of Corona-Virus helped some sectors of the economy such as Parcel Carriers, DIY Companies and Supermarkets. However, building construction is all but stopped and the Rope Access business has come to a virtual standstill.

At the time of writing this (July 2020) both the Caving and Rope Access business are extremely quiet and it is not possible to predict if or when customers might return in significant numbers to support a thriving business.

1972 – 2020 has been a lively time for Phil and his family, Phil & Chandra's two daughters each have two sons, giving the grandparents plenty to do helping keep them occupied. The oldest grandson is now nearing 175cm tall at age 15, (must have Phil's genes) Where they live not far from Buxton, they have a patio area which badly needed re-pointing with a brush in compound, sounds easy enough but first you have to jet the stone to clean it, kill any weeds with weed killer, and rake out all the old mortar. A very time consuming and potentially expensive job. Phil had the idea to supply the children with plugging chisels, hammers, safety visors and gloves, and they could keep themselves busy during school holidays. Wow, half the job was done in just a week, amazing, and valuable new skills learned not to mention the dogged determination needed to stick at it two hours a day.

Phil has personally kept extremely busy during the lockdown period, working at the shop catching up on building maintenance, keeping the shop open for essential business 10am – 4pm, working at the sewing machine making specialist commercial non caving products, and doing all the things necessary to keep a business functioning, before going home earlier than usual to fit new fence posts, build a new shed, and other DIY jobs around the home.

Today, Saturday 25th July 2020 the Covid-19 lockdown has been eased, normal life is slowly returning and people are legally required to wear face masks in shops. Two customers visited the shop today, and a few mail orders were taken during the week. It will be interesting to see how many shops survive the pandemic, the lockdown, and the inevitable aftermath of higher inflation and job losses. Life will no doubt get back to some kind of normal before too long, and we'll be able to say, "do you remember the Corona pandemic?"

CELEBRATIONS

Queen Elizabeth II Silver Jubilee Party 1977. Monsal Avenue.

Prince Charles' and Lady Diana's wedding day 1981. Queen's Road. Left to right Helen Smith, Rachel Goodwin, Helen Sleigh, Lisa Mulryan, Lynne Conneely, Ena Smith, Peter Smith, Yvette Gibson, Deborah Critchlow, Joanne Bagshaw, June Smith and Tracy Kidd.

COVID-19 SNAKE!

BE A GIVER NOT A TAKER!

IN OTHER WORDS, PLEASE DO NOT
REMOVE ANY STONES - ONLY ADD THEM...

WE DON'T WANT TO CONTRIBUTE TO
SPREADING THE VIRUS AND WE NEED OUR
SNAKE TO GROW!

Covid-19 Snake!

The Covid Snake, creator Clare Cartledge,
participants Uncle Tom Cobley and all.

Buxton - a community responds to a global pandemic

Caitlin Bisknell July 2020

As the lockdown restrictions look set to be re-introduced in some shape or form, it is difficult to comprehend what has happened over the past few weeks and months. Locally, nationally and internationally. But one thing is clear – Buxtonians reacted magnificently, once again proving what a hardy breed they are.

The changes to our everyday life have been immense, from being told not to go out unless absolutely necessary to today where wearing face coverings has become the norm.

Back in February 2020 I was busy planning a holiday and having just lost my job, I was wondering what to do with my spare time. By mid-March Corona virus had engulfed my life, and has not yet let go.

So what happened?

Alongside all of the concern and worry, a community movement, Buxton Street by Street Covid-19 support, took off. Set up on March 16 as Facebook group by local community nurse, Anna Watson. One soon became three when Claire Mitchell and I volunteered our services a few days later.

In the days before lockdown was introduced, Buxtonians were busy delivering leaflets to their neighbours, offering help to run errands or to stop by for a, socially distanced, chat. We knew that when lockdown became a reality, many people would be left isolated. They would need help to get shopping and medication, and they would also want a friendly chat.

Our leaflets offered local support – literally from a neighbour just down the road.

Buxton Street by Street grew rapidly. Within a couple of weeks we had recruited 200 volunteers and delivered nearly 10,000 flyers covering each of Buxton's 300-odd streets.

Soon we had a network of around 50 people who were regularly helping their neighbours s with shopping and other errands. All neatly organised into area-based WhatsApp groups – which acted as a support network for volunteers to ask questions and to share experiences; and to seek help if they became unwell.

Connex and High Peak CVS gave us a wealth of guidance and support, as we worked daily to meet the needs of local residents.

Before long, Richard Graham of Buxton Website Design set up a free website for us. We built links with Vision Buxton and Explore Buxton, Buxton Town Team and Buxton Rotary, and of course, High Peak Foodbank and Connex.

Later we joined forces with the volunteers of the For the Love of Scrubs Buxton group, using our delivery network to distribute locally made scrubs and PPE to health and social care providers to help them to stay safe.

Every day a welter of information – and some disinformation - was coming out from all kinds of sources. We used our Facebook page and website to highlight and to share officially recognised guidance and information, from public health information to shop opening hours.

By now the national NHS Volunteer Responders scheme had been set up to offer support including delivering food and medication and telephone befriending, but was struggling with the number of enquiries.

Back in Buxton we were already offering – and delivering - that service through our own volunteers, many of whom were also NHS Volunteers.

Locally, shops too adapted rapidly.

Potters and Hargreaves – mainstays of our local high street for so many years – closed their doors and seemingly went into enforced hibernation. But behind those doors – work was continuing apace.

Websites were updated, online shopping was promoted. And preparations started for the day when they would physically be allowed to re-open.

Over in the Cavendish Arcade, AtticusBoo kept us all amused with its daily updates and Jantar made the most of the enforced closure to set up a brand new website – photographing every item of jewellery in the store!

The borough council played its part too – distributing business grants in record time; even though most of its staff were working from home

Buxton Market – was one of the few markets that kept going – missing only one day's trading during lockdown. Yes, it was reduced to a single fruit and veg stall – but that stall rapidly attracted a growing number of customers. And with the lifting of restrictions Buxton Market has come back bigger and stronger than ever.

Food shops and cafés changed their ways of working to set up take away and delivery services.

While some had to furlough staff, others, like Mycocks Butchers, seemed busier than ever.

Outside supermarkets people queued patiently, come rain or shine – thankfully (and it has to be said a little unusually for Buxton) it was mostly shine.

Inside staff struggled to fill the shelves as people bulk bought pasta and loo roll – I still don't know why. As the pandemic continued people turned to baking and the shelves emptied of flour and sugar.

No matter what they did – whether, open or closed – they all played their part in keeping Buxton alive. Hopefully Buxtonians will continue to shop locally now that restrictions are lifting and shops are re-opening.

It was sadly inevitable that the 2020 Buxton International Festival was cancelled – another blow to our town's economy. But it too bounced back with online events – and even a socially distanced performance outside the Opera House.

The Fringe thrived with a mix of actual and virtual events, and some fantastic window displays of artwork. Not forgetting Floella who took up residence on Spring Gardens as part of the Sculpture Trail.

The Opera House looked magnificent bathed in red to highlight the impact that Covid-19 has had on all performing arts.

Lockdown also enabled many of us to discover, or re-discover, areas of the town we had not visited previously or for a long time. The understated beauty of Ashwood Park; the glorious bluebells in Corbar Wood; the delights in, around and above the former Lightwood Reservoir. All accessible from our home.

Throughout all of this our keyworkers: nurses, doctors, ambulance crews, care home and social care staff, teachers and school staff continued to work. Putting their lives at risk each and every day.

We owe a huge debt of gratitude to all of them for so selflessly stepping up – the Thursday evening 'Clap for our Keyworkers' now a distant memory, hardly seemed enough.

As we all long for a return to some new kind of normality, the yearning to hug our loved ones grows even stronger and harder to ignore.

As individuals, and as community, we have shown that we have the resilience and ability to look after our neighbour's and our community. Long may that spirit continue.

09/10/20

Stop Press: Just as this book was going to print, Buxton Street By Street and Connex had confirmation that their funding bid to the National Lottery Fund for a grant to continue to build community resilience in Buxton had been successful.

Future plans and ideas include:

- Working with young people and schools to identify the impact lockdown and separation has had on mental wellbeing.

- Continuing to work with High Peak Foodbank and its partner organisation Zink Employability and Advice to help people who are in hardship.

- Finding ways use the internet to support people who want to stay at home, using the internet to reduce isolation during lockdown.

- Helping people to overcome anxiety about going out.

Where is everybody?

Facebook posting May 2020

Vicki Zoppi

Ok, my van will be out and about from 1.30 calling at Sylvan Cliff, Curzon Road, Kedleston Road, Batham Gate Road, Peak Dale, Dove, and Chapel en Le Frith. Listen out for it.

28th May, Dad is out and about on Otterhole then Carr Road, Turner Road, then Hogshaw, Nunsfield Road, Brown Edge Road, then Fairfield.

Snippet

Vincenzo Zoppi started the family business in 1967.

Snippet

Posted through my letter box.

Hello!

During the coming weeks if there is anything you need urgently- such as food, a prescription collecting or to find out information which you can't without using the internet or you just need someone to talk to,

please call me, Gary

HELLO! **If you are self-isolating, I can help.**

My name is
....

I live locally at
....

My phone number is
....

If you are self-isolating due to COVID-19 I can help with:

☐ Picking up shopping   ☐ Posting mail

☐ A friendly phone call   ☐ Urgent supplies

Just call or text me and I'll do my best to help you (for free!)

Coronavirus is contagious. Please take every precaution to ensure you are spreading only kindness. Avoid physical contact (2m distance). Wash your hands regularly. Items should be left on your doorstep. **#ViralKindness**

Photo by John Bradburn.

ACKNOWLEDGEMENTS

This has been tough crossing the completion line. What with covid 'n' all. Good job I started it in 2018.

I wish to thank all of you who contributed your written and dictated stories, tales and anecdotes.

Those of you, I have mentioned from the social media, local topics, sites.

Staff at Buxton Library who have been patient, helpful and welcoming.

Chris Bradburn and Robbie Jones for being there, helping with proof reading and guidance.

Martin Elvin for graciously letting me use his dad's cartoons.

White Hall and Eldon Pothole club for the photographs.

Kevin Hall for allowing me to plonk him on the back cover.

Thanks also those of you who unwittingly gave me a snippet in conversation.

Due to the nature of the book, my apologies for any dates, names and facts that are incorrect due to memory.

As Rag 'n' Bone Man's lyrics go "I'm only human after all".

Finally, thank you to Printexpress. We did it!

Yvonne

Email: yvonneechalker@aolmail.com